Strategy

Harvard Business Essentials

The New Manager's Guide and Mentor

The Harvard Business Essentials series is designed to provide comprehensive advice, personal coaching, background information, and guidance on the most relevant topics in business. Drawing on rich content from Harvard Business School Publishing and other sources, these concise guides are carefully crafted to provide a highly practical resource for readers with all levels of experience, and will prove especially valuable for the new manager. To assure quality and accuracy, each volume is closely reviewed by a specialized content adviser from a world-class business school. Whether you are a new manager seeking to expand your skills or a seasoned professional looking to broaden your knowledge base, these solution-oriented books put reliable answers at your fingertips.

Other books in the series:

Finance for Managers
Hiring and Keeping the Best People
Managing Change and Transition
Negotiation
Business Communication
Managing Projects Large and Small
Manager's Toolkit
Crisis Management
Entrepreneur's Toolkit
Time Management
Power, Influence, and Persuasion

Strategy

Create and Implement the Best
Strategy for Your Business

Harvard Business School Press | *Boston, Massachusetts*

Library of Congress Cataloging-in-Publication Data
Harvard business essentials : strategy : create and implement
the best strategy for your business.
p. cm. — (Harvard business essentials)
Includes bibliographical references and index.
ISBN 1-59139-632-8
1. Strategic planning. 2. Business planning. I. Title: Strategy.
II. Title: Strategy, create and implement the best strategy for your business.
III. Harvard Business School. IV. Series: Harvard business essentials series.
HD30.28.H3785 2005
658.4'012—dc22
2005000767

Contents

Introduction   **xi**

1   **SWOT Analysis I**   **1**
Looking Outside for Threats and Opportunities

    External Analysis   3
    Porter's Five Forces Framework   13
    Summing Up   15

2   **SWOT Analysis II**   **17**
Looking Inside for Strengths and Weaknesses

    Core Competencies   18
    Financial Condition   23
    Management and Culture   24
    A Method for Evaluating Internal Strengths and Weaknesses   25
    Summing Up   27

3   **Types of Strategy**   **29**
Which Fits Your Business?

    Low-Cost Leadership   31
    Differentiation   36
    Customer Relationship   38
    Network Effect Strategy   42
    Summing Up   45

4   Strategic Moves   **47**
The Mechanisms of Success

    Gaining a Market Beachhead   48
    Market Entry Through Process Innovation   50
    Applying Judo Strategy   52
    Market Entry Through Product Differentiation   54
    Create and Dominate a New Market   55
    Buying Your Way In   57
    Summing Up   59

5   From Strategy to Implementation   **61**
Seeking Alignment

    People and Incentives   66
    Supportive Activities   68
    Organizational Structure   70
    Culture and Leadership   71
    Summing Up   75

6   Action Plans   **77**
The Architecture of Implementation

    From Strategic Plan to Unit Action Plans   78
    Set Goals   80
    Agree on Performance Measures   82
    Formulate Action Steps   84
    Determine the Resources Needed   85
    Identify Interlocks   86
    Estimate the Financial Impact   90
    A Sample Action Plan   90
    Summing Up   92

7   How to Stay on Course   **95**
Sensing and Responding to Deviations from Plan

    A Model for Staying on Course   96
    Progress Review   98
    Informal Checks   101
    Common Causes of Implementation Failure   102

Develop Contingency Plans to Handle Potential Setbacks 106

Summing Up 108

8 The People Side of Implementation **109**

Getting the Right People on Board

Enlist the Support and Involvement of Key People 111

Support the Plan with Consistent Behaviors and Messages 113

Develop Enabling Structures 114

Celebrate Milestones 115

Communicate Relentlessly 117

Summing Up 120

9 Strategy as Work-in-Progress **121**

Keep Looking Ahead

How Well Is Your Strategy Working? 123

Warning Signs 130

Leading Strategic Change 134

Summing Up 135

Appendix: Useful Implementation Tools **137**

Notes **141**

Glossary **145**

For Further Reading **149**

Index **157**

About the Subject Adviser **161**

About the Writer **162**

Strategy

Introduction

This book is about strategy creation and implementation. A good strategy matched with outstanding implementation is every company's best assurance of success. It is also an undeniable sign of good management. As an Essentials publication, this book does not cover everything in depth, and it certainly won't make you a strategy expert. But it does address all the important topics, and will get you off to a very good start—and with substantial confidence.

Strategy creation is about *doing the right things* and is a primary concern of senior executives and business owners. Implementation is about *doing things right,* a much different set of activities. Both senior executives and lower-ranking managers must give implementation intense attention, since even a great strategy is worthless if people fail to implement it properly. Yet, oddly, much has been written about business strategy but far less has been written about implementation. We hope to correct that problem in the chapters that follow.

What Is Strategy?

In its original sense, strategy (from the Greek word, *strategos*) is a military term used to describe the art of the general. It refers to the general's plan for arraying and maneuvering his forces with the goal of defeating an enemy army. Carl von Clausewitz, the nineteenth-century theoretician of the art of war, described strategy as "concerned with drafting the plan of war and shaping the individual campaigns, and within these, deciding on the individual engagements."[1] More recently, in the era when nation states are pitted against each other, the concept of strategy has broadened. Historian Edward Mead Earle describes it as "the art of controlling and utilizing the resources of a nation—or a coalition of nations—including its armed forces, to the end that its vital interests shall be effectively promoted and secured."[2]

Businesspeople have always liked military analogies, so it is not surprising that they have embraced the notion of strategy. They too began to think of strategy as a plan for controlling and utilizing their resources (human, physical, and financial) with the goal of promoting and securing their vital interests. Kenneth Andrews was the first to articulate these emerging ideas in his classic, *The Concept of Corporate Strategy*, published in 1971. Andrews described a framework that remains useful today, defining strategy in terms of what a business can do—that is, its strengths and weaknesses—and what possibilities are open to it—that is, the outer environment of opportunities and threats.[3] A decade or so later, Harvard professor Michael Porter sharpened this definition, describing strategy as "a broad formula for how a business is going to compete."[4]

Bruce Henderson, founder of The Boston Consulting Group, and one of the tribal elders of corporate strategy, connected the notion of strategy with competitive advantage, perhaps borrowing a concept drawn from economics (comparative advantage). A *competitive advantage* is a function of strategy that puts a firm in a better position than rivals to create economic value for customers. Henderson wrote that "Strategy is a deliberate search for a plan of action that will develop a business's competitive advantage and compound it." Competitive advantage, he went on, is founded in differences. "The differences between you and your competitors are the basis of your advantage."[5]

Henderson believes that no two competitors could coexist if both sought to do business in the same way. They must differentiate themselves to survive. "Each must be different enough to have a unique advantage." For example, two men's clothing stores on the same block—one featuring formal attire and the other focusing on leisure wear—could potentially survive and prosper. Their physical proximity might even create mutual benefits. However, if the same two stores were to sell the same things under the same terms, one or the other would perish. Faced with this situation, each would attempt to differentiate itself in ways most pleasing to customers—through price, product mix, or ambiance.

Michael Porter concurs with Henderson's idea of being different: "Competitive strategy is about being different. It means deliberately choosing a different set of activities to deliver a unique mix of value."[6] Consider these familiar examples:

- Southwest Airlines didn't become the most profitable air carrier in North America by copying its rivals. It differentiated itself with a strategy characterized by low fares, frequent departures, point-to-point service, and customer-pleasing service.

- eBay created a different way for people to sell and acquire goods: online auctions. Company founders aimed to serve the same purpose as classified ads, flea markets, and formal auctions, but made it simple, efficient, and wide-reaching. Online auctions have differentiated the company's service from those of traditional competitors.

- Toyota's strategy in developing the hybrid engine Prius passenger car was to create a competitive advantage in the eyes of an important segment of auto buyers: people who want a vehicle that is environmentally benign, cheap to operate, and/or the latest thing in auto engineering.

So far, these strategies have served their initiators very well and have provided competitive advantages over rivals. Southwest is the most profitable U.S. air carrier, eBay is the most successful Internet company ever, and, at this writing, Toyota has a four-month waiting list of customers for its hybrid car. Being different can take many forms. As we'll see later, even companies whose products are identical to their competitors' can strategically set themselves apart by, for example, offering a better price or by providing faster and more reliable delivery.

Being "different," of course, does not in itself confer competitive advantage or assure business success. A rocket car would be "different" but would be unlikely to attract enough customers to be successful. A hybrid (gasoline/electric) powered car, in contrast, is different in a way that creates superior value for customers in terms of fuel economy and low exhaust emissions. Those are values for which customers will gladly pay.

So, what is strategy? *Strategy* is a plan that aims to give the enterprise a competitive advantage over rivals through differentiation. Strategy is about understanding what you do, what you want to become, and—most importantly—focusing on how you plan to get there. Likewise, it is about what you *don't* do; it draws boundaries around the scope of a company's intentions. A sound strategy, skillfully implemented, identifies the goals and direction that managers and employees at every level need in order to define their work and make their organization successful. An organization without a clear strategy, in contrast, is rudderless. It flails about, dashing off in one direction after another as opportunities present themselves, but never achieving a great deal.

Strategy operates at both corporate and operating unit levels. For example, General Electric consists of many divisions operating in different industries: aircraft engines, home appliances, capital services, lighting, medical systems, plastics, power systems, and electrical distribution and control. It even owns NBC, one of the major U.S. television networks. The people who run this vast enterprise have a strategy, as do the senior managers of each division. Because the divisions operate in very different industries and competitive environments, their strategies must, of necessity, be unique. But each must be aligned with the larger corporate strategy.

Strategy Versus Business Model

Many confuse strategy with a newly popular term: *business model*. That expression first came into popular use in the late 1980s, at a time when people were gaining experience with personal computers and spreadsheet software. Thanks to these software innovations, businesspeople found that they could easily "model" the costs and revenues associated with any proposed business. After the model was set up, it took only a few keystrokes to observe the impact of individual changes—for example, in unit price, profit margin, and supplier costs—on the bottom line. Pro forma financial statements were the primary documents of business modeling. By the time dot-com fever had become rampant, the term was a popular buzzword. Still, most people were unable to articulate exactly what it meant.

Scholars define a business model as the economic underpinnings of an enterprise's strategy. Management consultant Joan Magretta has provided a useful introduction to business models in "Why Business Models Matter," a 2002 *Harvard Business Review* article in which she describes a business model as some variation of the value chain that supports every business. "Broadly speaking," she writes, "this chain has two parts. Part one includes all the activities associated with making something: designing it, purchasing raw materials, manufacturing, and so on. Part two includes all the activities associated with selling something: finding and reaching customers, transacting a sale, distributing the product or delivering the service."[7] Thus, the business model is more about the mechanisms through which the entity produces and delivers a product or service, and less about what differentiates it in the eyes of customers and gives it competitive advantage. It answers these questions: How does this thing work? What underlying economic logic explains how we can deliver value to customers at an appropriate cost?

Every viable organization is built on a sound business model, but a business model isn't a strategy, even though many people use the terms interchangeably. Business models describe, as a system, how the pieces of a business fit together to produce a profit. But they don't factor in a critical dimension of performance: competition. That's the job of strategy.

Some of today's most powerful and profitable companies grew out of business models that were elegant and compelling in their logic and powerful in economic potential. Dell Computer is one of these and the most often-cited example.

eBay, the online auction company, is another such example. It grew out of a very simple and traditional model. Like a long-distance telephone company, eBay created an infrastructure that allowed people to communicate; and, again like the long-distance provider, it picked up a modest fee from each use. Its Web-based infrastructure of software, servers, and rules of behavior allows a community of buyers and sellers to meet and conduct transactions for all manner of goods—from Elvis memorabilia to used Porsches. The company takes no part in the transactions, thereby avoiding many of the costs incurred by other businesses. Its only responsibilities are to maintain the integrity of the auction process and the information system that make its auctions possible.

As a mechanism for generating income, the eBay model is simple. It receives revenues from seller fees. Those revenues are reduced by the cost of building and maintaining the online infrastructure and by the usual marketing, product development, general, and administrative costs that keep the operation running and that attract buyers and sellers to the site. The net of these revenues and costs is profits for eBay shareholders.

Aside from its simplicity, the great power of the eBay model is the fact that a small number of salaried employees and outsource partners can handle a huge and growing volume of business. Further, a doubling of transaction volume (and revenue) can be accommodated with relatively modest investments. Software and servers do the heavy lifting. This activity is much different from the company's stated strategy, which is to build and effectively support the world's most efficient and abundant Web-based marketplace—a marketplace in which anyone, anywhere, can buy or sell almost anything.

As this example should make clear, strategy and business models are different concepts, even though they are related. While strategy provides differentiation and competitive advantage, the business model explains the economics of how the business works and makes money.

The Strategy Process

Like most important things in business, strategy creation and its implementation should be approached as a process, that is, as a set of activities that transforms inputs into outputs. This process is described graphically in figure I-1. Here we see that strategy creation follows from the mission of the company, which defines its purpose and what it aims to do for customers and other stakeholders. Given the mission, senior management sets goals—tangible manifestations of the organization's mission that are used to measure progress. Goals, as shown in the figure, should be informed by a pragmatic understanding of both the external business/market environment and the internal capabilities of the organization.

Strategy creation typically begins with extensive research and analysis and a process through which senior management zeros in on the top priority issues that the company needs to tackle to be successful in the long term. For each priority issue, units and teams are asked to create high-level action plans. Once these action plans are developed, the company's high-level strategic objectives and direction statement are further clarified.

FIGURE I-1

The Strategy Process

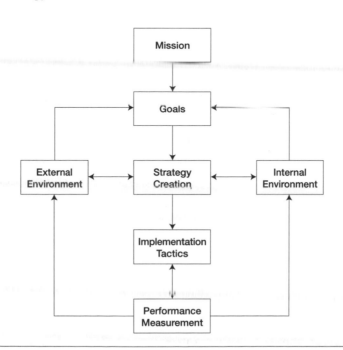

Strategic creation takes time and requires a series of back-and-forth communications between senior management and operating units, whereby all parties examine, discuss, and refine the plan. As a result, various planning streams often happen in parallel. The importance of involvement of operating units in the strategic planning processes cannot be overemphasized. Operating units house tremendous knowledge about their own capabilities and the competitive environments in which they operate. People in the operating units can make informed recommendations about what the company should be doing and where it should be going. Furthermore, units that are included in the planning process are more likely to support and implement the plans that are created. Units are the implementation centers of an organization. They have the leadership, people, and skills needed for effective execution. Organizations that fail to include units in the strategic planning process typically receive results inferior to those that do.

By undertaking the planning process together, senior management and unit leaders ensure that a company's strategies—corporate and unit—are tightly aligned and that successful implementation can follow.

What's Ahead

Strategy begins with goals, which follow naturally from the entity's mission. Goals, in turn, are influenced by an iterative sensing of the external environment and the organization's internal capabilities. The strategic choices available to a company likewise emerge from the process of looking outside and inside. Strategic planners refer to this activity as SWOT analysis: *S*trengths, *W*eaknesses, *O*pportunities, and *T*hreats. Chapter 1 will help you examine the external environment of opportunities and threats. Chapter 2 turns the focus inward, to the strengths and weaknesses of the enterprise. Knowledge of this inner world imparts a practical sense about what company goals and what strategies are most feasible and promising. The chapter's emphasis is on the most important areas in which a company's strengths and weaknesses should be evaluated: core competencies and processes, financial condition, and management and culture.

Once you've gotten a clear sense of your company's strengths and weaknesses and the external environment in which you must operate, the question is, "What type of strategy should we pursue?" There are many strategy "types" from which to choose. Chapter 3 describes four generic types and what it takes to succeed with each: low-cost leadership, product/service differentiation, customer relationship, and network effect. Chances are that one of these—or some variation thereof—will be appropriate for your company and give it a defensible and profitable hold on some segment of the market.

Chapter 4 continues the discussion, indicating how strategy can be used to enter and build defensible positions in the marketplace. It explores a number of potential strategic moves: creating a market beachhead, using innovation to overcome barriers to entry, the principles of *judo strategy*, and others.

Having a great strategy is only part of the challenge. Equal or greater attention must be given to implementation, the many measures that translate strategic intent into actions that produce results. Chapter 5 takes us from strategy creation to the first steps of strategy implementation. It explains the need for alignment between strategy and the day-to-day details of how your company operates. Successful alignment and implementation begins with action plans developed and executed at the unit level. Chapter 6 segments the action-planning process into a number of key steps. It also contains an example of one company's formal action plan.

Chapter 7 is about keeping action plans on track. Managers cannot simply issue a set of instructions and expect flawless implementation. Instead, they must support their plans with consistent behaviors, training, and other reinforcing. And they must communicate relentlessly with respect to the nature of the strategy and its benefits to everyone in the company.

People are the most important part of implementation. Harnessing their energy and commitment to strategic change is often management's greatest challenge. Employees must feel that they've had something to say about the plans they are told to implement. They must know that success is important to their personal careers and fortunes. They must be motivated to do the right things well. And they must see real incentives for all their hard work. Chapter 8 addresses each of these requirements.

No strategy, even a great one, remains effective forever. Something in the environment eventually changes, rendering the current strategy ineffective or unprofitable. Leaders must be alert to these changes. Chapter 9 explains how managers can assess the effectiveness of their current strategies and recognize when they are losing the power to capture and satisfy customers. It offers tips on how they can monitor the performance of their strategies and identify areas where their intervention is necessary.

That's it for the book's chapters. But the end matter contains material you may also find useful. First, there is an appendix, which contains the following items:

- **Worksheet for Conducting a SWOT Analysis.** SWOT analysis, as described in chapters 1 and 2, is used by strategic planners to identify the company's strengths, weaknesses, opportunities, and threats. This worksheet can help you to be systematic in thinking about and evaluating these internal and external factors. Free copies of this worksheet can be downloaded from the Harvard Business Essentials series Web site: www.elearning .hbsp.org/businesstools. You'll also find other useful management and financial tools on that site.

- **Worksheet for Work Breakdown Structure (WBS).** Work breakdown structure, borrowed from the art and science of project management, is one of the implementation tools described in the text. You can use this worksheet to deconstruct large tasks into their component parts and to estimate the time needed to complete them. This worksheet is also downloadable from the series Web site.

- **Project Progress Report.** If you treat your strategy implementation as a project, you'll find this a useful tool for noting progress to key milestones, key decisions, and budget status. It is downloadable from the series Web site.

The worksheet appendix is followed by a glossary of terms particular to strategy creation and implementation. Every business activity has its specialized vocabulary, and this one is no different. When you see a term in italics, that's your cue that it's included in the glossary.

A final section identifies readily available books and articles that can tell you more about topics covered in this book. Being an Essentials book, this volume cannot cover everything you might want to know about strategy creation and implementation, so if you want to know more, refer to the publications listed in this section.

The content of this book draws heavily on the strategy scholarship published in books and articles over the past twenty-four years. Many of these first appeared as articles in the *Harvard Business Review*. For material on strategy implementation, some of the best material was found in Harvard ManageMentor® on Implementing Strategy, an on-line service of Harvard Business School Publishing. All other sources are noted with standard endnote citations.

1

SWOT Analysis I

Looking Outside for Threats and Opportunities

Key Topics Covered in This Chapter

- *Identifying threats and opportunities in the external environment*

- *The world of workstyle and lifestyle trends that can affect your business*

- *Assessing customers*

- *Changes in the competitive arena*

- *Porter's five forces framework*

STRATEGY BEGINS WITH goals, which naturally follow from an entity's mission. But for practical purposes goals cannot stand in isolation. They are informed by an iterative sensing of the external environment and the organization's internal capabilities. As much as some may think that everything devolves from goals, the fact is that practical people form goals based on what is feasible, given the environment in which they must operate their own resources and capabilities. For example, 3M Corporation has committed itself to annual numerical goals: 10 percent earning growth or better, 27 percent return on employed capital, and so forth. Those specific goals didn't come out of a hat; they are a product of the insights of 3M executives and directors who understand the markets they serve and the capabilities of the company. They looked outside and inside to determine those goals.

As shown in figure 1-1, the strategic choices available to the enterprise likewise emerge from the process of looking outside and inside. Among strategic planners, this analysis goes by the acronym SWOT: *S*trengths, *W*eaknesses, *O*pportunities, and *T*hreats.

- **Strengths** are capabilities that enable your company or unit to perform well—capabilities that need to be leveraged.

- **Weaknesses** are characteristics that prohibit your company or unit from performing well and need to be addressed.

- **Opportunities** are trends, forces, events, and ideas that your company or unit can capitalize on.

FIGURE 1-1

External and Internal Analysis

External Analysis	Specific Goals	Internal Analysis
• Customers • Pricing constraints • Competitors • Distribution issues • Technology • Macroeconomy • Regulation • Workstyle trends • Major uncertainties • Suppliers • Potential partners **Threats and Opportunities**	**Strategy Formulation**	• Current performance • Brand power • Cost structure • Product portfolio • R&D pipeline • Technical mastery • Employee skills • Company culture **Strengths and Weaknesses**

- **Threats** are possible events or forces outside of your control that your company or unit needs to plan for or decide how to mitigate.

Considering both external and internal factors is essential because they clarify the world in which the business or the unit operates, enabling it to better envision its desired future. This chapter explains the first of these challenges: external analysis. We'll take up internal analysis later.

External Analysis

"The essence of formulating competitive strategy," writes scholar Michael Porter, "is relating a company to its environment."[1] Every company's environment is populated with customers, competitors, suppliers, and, in most cases, regulators. And all have an impact on its profit potential. There are both current and potential customers, each with requirements for product/service quality, features, and utility. Are any of these requirements unserved? There is also a set of current competitors and still others who might enter the arena.

Technology is part of the competitive environment, and that technology is always changing. Is there something developing in the world of technology that could alter your competitive environment, perhaps making the products of today's industry leaders obsolete?

Substitutes represent another threat factor in the external environment. For example, in the early 1980s, newly developed word-processing software for personal computers represented a substitute for the typewriter. The substitution rate was so rapid that typewriters were largely displaced within ten years. The current popularity of cell phones with digital imaging capabilities likewise has created a substitute for cameras and film. What are the potential substitutes for your products? Do any of your products have substitute potential in other markets?

An analysis of the external factors listed in the left-hand box of figure 1-1 helps the strategist to uncover and understand threats and opportunities, which, in turn, helps to reveal a company's strategic options. (This list is by no means exhaustive, and the reader is encouraged to think of other factors that pertain to his or her industry.) Because detailed coverage of each of these is beyond the scope of this Essentials book, we will address just a handful here. We will also discuss Michael Porter's "five forces" approach to analyzing competition in an industry, a conceptualization that has proven its value to business people for more than twenty-five years. (Note: For a more complete discussion of external analysis, see texts listed in the "For Further Reading" section at the back of this book. In particular, refer to Michael Porter, *Competitive Strategy*; David Aaker, *Developing Business Strategies*; and Jay Barney, *Gaining and Sustaining Competitive Advantage*.)

Workstyle and Lifestyle Trends

No matter what industry you're in, workstyle and lifestyle trends are likely to affect your future. Consider this one: According to IDC, a private research firm, the number of U.S. employees working on the road increased to 40 percent in 2004 and may rise to 66 percent by the end of 2006. Depending on your business, that raw statistic should provoke a number of questions:

- How will these millions of people travel?

- Where and what will they eat?

- Where will they spend the night, and what special accommodations would make evenings on the road more tolerable?

- How will they keep in touch with their families, offices, and clients while traveling?

- What can be done to reduce the cost of so much travel?

- How can wasted travel time be turned into productive time?

These are the kinds of questions for which executives in travel, restaurant, hospitality, and mobile computing and telecommunications industries should seek answers. Those answers will reveal threats for some and opportunities for others. For example, IDC's projection of increasing business travel is good news for airlines and hotels that cater to this segment of travelers. But it is also good news for companies that provide effective travel substitutes, such as Web- and videoconferencing products and services, and the success of these latter substitutes is a direct threat to those same airlines and hotels. Why spend piles of money and eat up productive time flying people to meetings when they could meet online or from videoconferencing facilities near home?

The growth in business travel is just one of many workstyle and lifestyle changes that are happening right under our noses. Each represents some combination of threat and opportunity to companies in a range of industries. Consider these:

- More and more people are working from home offices. These people rely heavily on telecommunications, PCs, and Internet connectivity. Their office-bound managers are not sure how to supervise them. How will these facts affect your business or provide opportunities for new business?

- The Internet has made shopping, research, arranging travel, and money management faster and more convenient. Will this kill your current business or open new opportunities to serve customers profitably?

- U.S. officials have declared obesity a national health epidemic, and EU citizens are also getting more portly. What does this declaration portend for food companies, restaurant chains, health clinics, and weight-control specialists?

- The price of new and older homes has exploded along the east and west coasts of the United States, putting home ownership out of reach for a growing number of people, and there is no relief in sight. What does this mean for new homebuilders, for building materials suppliers, and mortgage finance companies? Is there an opportunity here for a new approach to building and financing affordable housing?

- The populations of Europe and Japan are aging, and women of childbearing age in these countries are having fewer children. This will have huge implications for medical care systems, housing for the elderly, and labor markets. Strains on social services and pension systems are inevitable. Transitions like this contain threats for some companies and tremendous opportunities for others.

These are just a few of the many developments that are altering our world. Each is forcing companies to reformulate their strategies. So keep abreast of reports from think tanks, from IDC, Forrester Research, government agencies, and other investigative organizations. Scan many papers and periodicals. Conduct your own research into trends that may affect your business and form the basis of a new strategy. Pay particular attention to any area in which significant change is under way. Be broad-ranging in your scanning; the changes that affect you the most may be brewing outside your industry.

Customers

A business, as Peter Drucker once wrote, has no higher requirement than that to create customers. In the absence of customers, the many things that businesses do—product development, manufacturing, shipping, and so forth—are utterly pointless. Thus, analysis of external factors generally begins with a study of customers:

- Who are they?
- How sensitive are they to price?
- How can they be reached?
- How are they currently using a particular product or service?
- Which of their needs are poorly served—or unserved?
- What level of loyalty do they have to current vendors?
- Do they seek an arm's-length transaction or a long-term relationship?

Since potential questions about customers are so numerous, it's useful to segment customers into groups that have common features. *Market segmentation* comes directly from the marketer's toolkit; it is a technique for dividing a large heterogeneous market of customers into smaller segments with homogeneous features. Those homogeneous features many be defined in any number of ways. Here are some examples:

- **Age**—senior citizens, teenagers, college students
- **Gender**—women, foreign-born men
- **Geographic location**—suburban families north and west of London
- **Type of users**—heavy users of voice messaging, lead users
- **Income**—households with total incomes between € 30,000 and € 50,000
- **Behavior**—people who shop regularly via the Internet

Analysis of customer segments has many uses for strategists. Segmentation makes it easier to identify the needs (met and unmet), price sensitivity, accessibility, and loyalty of identifiable customers. The study of key segments may, for example, reveal that some customers are much more profitable to serve than others. For instance, during the early days of the cell-phone era, research by one firm uncovered several distinct customers segments:

- **Infrequent users.** These were people (mostly women) who subscribed at the minimum level and mostly for personal safety reasons. This segment bought the lowest-price service and was unprofitable to serve. Turnover in the segment was extremely high as these customers switched service providers in response to special, low-priced deals offered periodically by rivals.

- **Occasional users.** These were customers who made only a few calls each week. The cell-phone company broke even on this group.

- **Business professionals.** These people used their cell phones regularly and subscribed to the premium services. They were also loyal and relatively insensitive to prices. Most of the company's profits came from this segment.

These findings had an impact on the telecom company's future strategy.

Take a few minutes to think about the customers in your industry—both the ones you have and the ones you'd like to recruit. How much does your company really know about these people and their needs? Has it segmented them into homogeneous groups that reveal key facts for strategists? Are any important and potentially profitable segments unserved by you or your competitors?

Price Sensitivity and Elasticity of Demand

Among the external factors that strategists should understand is the price sensitivity of customers. Whether they intend to offer customers a new disk drive, a low-carbohydrate family of snack foods, or a new drug therapy, they must have an informed awareness of the relationship between price and customer demand.

A basic tenet of economics in a free market is that people will buy more of a good or service when the price goes down, and less as the price rises, all other factors remaining unchanged. This is both intuitively obvious and easily substantiated. Rational consumers are sensitive to price. Figure 1-2 shows the elasticity of demand for two products. The sharp slope in the demand curve (D) for Product A indicates a high sensitivity to a price increase; customers will make many fewer purchases as the price increases. Product B, in contrast, demonstrates much less sensitivity to a price increase; customers reduce their purchase only slightly in the face of rising prices; as economists would say, demand is relatively inelastic.

Some goods and services demonstrate relatively low price sensitivity—at least in the short term. Consider automobile fuel. The 30 percent rise in U.S. gasoline prices in the fall of 2004, when crude oil skyrocketed to $54 per barrel, caused only a 2 to 3 percent drop in U.S. gasoline consumption. Why? People were so locked into vacation plans and commuting routines that the increase caused little more than a ripple in demand. If that level of pricing (or rising prices) were to persist for a long time, however, consumption would drop substantially as people stopped buying gas-guzzling SUVs, opted to use public transportation, began carpooling to work, and so forth. As if to confirm this long-term effect, OPEC, the cartel of oil-producing countries, intimated that it wanted to see crude prices to return to the $22- to $25 per barrel range. Though the spurt in prices was a huge

FIGURE 1-2

Sensitivity to Price Changes

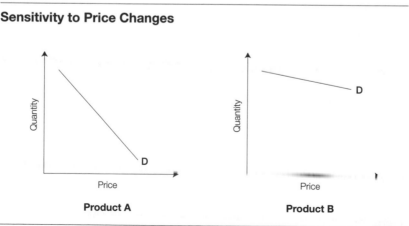

Product A   Product B

windfall for OPEC members, they knew that sustained high prices would induce their customers to find substitutes for petroleum and to invest seriously in alternative energy sources—hurting oil producers in the long run.

Many products and services exhibit a much more immediate and dramatic response to price changes, usually because the product or service is nonessential or because it has many available substitutes. Beef is an example. Every time that the price of beef has increased sharply, demand has declined immediately and almost as dramatically. Shoppers look at the price and say, "I think we'll have chicken for dinner tonight."

Economists use the term *price elasticity of demand* to quantify the impact of price changes on customer demands. If you've taken microeconomics, you are probably familiar with this concept. Price elasticity of demand is calculated as follows:

Percentage increase in price/Percentage decrease in quantity
= Price elasticity of demand

Thus, if a company raised the price of a product price from $100 to $120, price would increase by 20 percent. If that increase caused the quantity sold to drop from 600 units to 550 units, the percentage decrease would be 8.3 percent. Following our formula, the price elasticity of demand would be

20/8.3 = 2.4

The higher the final number, the more sensitive customers are to price changes.

Knowing how customers will respond to a price change can often be determined by means of focus groups, questionnaires, and direct experiments in local markets. For example, the producer of a breakfast cereal sold throughout the EU might raise its price in Brussels and observe the impact on unit sales.

To complete this analysis, however, the strategist should calculate the anticipated impact of a price change on total revenue. People may be buying fewer items at a higher price. For the example just given, the company had been selling 600 units at $100 each, earning revenues of $60,000. Under its new scenario, it expects to sell 550 units at $120, resulting in total revenue of $66,000. Further analysis would be needed to determine if that higher revenue figure translated into higher or lower gross profits.

Formal studies of price elasticity of demand are normally reserved for tactical moves. Nevertheless, understanding the relationship between price levels and customer buying behavior is an important piece of the larger puzzle that strategists must understand.

How well do you understand customer price sensitivity in your markets? How does that understanding inform your strategic choices?

The Competitive Arena

As George Day, a professor at the Wharton School, has perceptively written, "One of the primary issues facing mangers in formulating competitive strategy is defining the arena of competition. Where are you competing? Who are your competitors? How attractive is the competitive arena?"[2] No examination of the external environment is complete without a thoughtful analysis of competitors and the competitive arena. You surely know who your competitors are. They are the ones your salespeople wrestle with every day in closing key sales. They are the companies that aim to steal your best customers. Yes, you know who they are, but how much do you know *about* them—their strengths and weaknesses? Are you aware of emerging arenas of competition? And what about the competitors who will appear in the months and years ahead?

Some arenas of competition are relatively static, particularly in mature, capital-intensive industries. The steel industry up until the 1970s could be defined as static. A handful of large competitors were slugging it out, each trying to lower unit production costs and capture a larger slice of the market at the expense of its rivals. Other industries are more dynamic. The entertainment industry is a prime example. Twenty years ago, people in the United States could watch three or four network television stations, a public station, and one or two local stations. They could also go to a movie theater, or attend a live performance. Today, TV viewers can still watch network channels, but can also access hundreds of cable channels. The movie theaters are still there, but thousands of movies are now available through VHS, DVD, cable, and pay-per-view outlets. Because many of these entertainment services are vulnerable to substitution by others, vendors are scratching their head and asking, "What strategy will help us carve out a profitable niche in this dynamic marketplace? And what's coming next?"

The hallmarks of a dynamic market include:

- Many different products/services addressing a similar need (e.g., land line phones, cell phones, instant messaging, e-mail)

- A diversity of competitors (e.g., TV networks, cable companies, video rental shops, live venues)

- Few insurmountable barriers to entry

- Market fragmentation

How well do you understand competition in the market you aim to serve? Few areas of research provide greater dividends for strategists than this one.

Emerging Technology

Technology is a major driver of the modern economy. Intel, Cisco Systems, Siemens, and Genzyme have made their way in the world by creating and harnessing new or improved technologies. eBay, Amazon.com, Google, Cingular, and Yahoo! wouldn't even exist if computers and Internet technologies had not been developed. Even your local grocery store, a very traditional business, relies on technology to speed check-out lines, reduce errors, track sales by category, and manage its inventory.

Technology represents both a threat and an opportunity. It is a threat in the sense that a new technology may undermine your existing business, just as word-processing software and PCs torpedoed the typewriter industry, and as digital imaging is currently undermining the photographic film/film-processing business today. Putting the shoe on the other foot, we know that technology can provide powerful opportunities for companies that commercialize it in ways that provide clear benefits and value to customers.

Porter's Five Forces Framework

No discussion of the competitive environment would be complete without some discussion of Michael Porter's five forces framework. First articulated in 1979 in an award-winning *Harvard Business Review* article on "How Competitive Forces Shape Strategy," Porter's framework remains a useful tool for getting an analytical grasp on the state of competition and the underlying economics within an industry. It also encourages the strategist to look outside the small circle of current competing rivals to other actors and influences that determine potential profitability and growth. Porter identified the following forces as governing industry competition (see figure 1-3):

- Threat of new entrants

- Bargaining power of suppliers

FIGURE 1-3

Porter's Five Forces

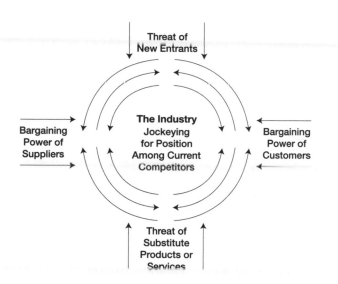

Source: Michael E. Porter, "How Competitive Forces Shape Strategy," *Harvard Business Review,* March–April 1979, 141. Reproduced with permission.

- Jockeying for position among current competitors

- Bargaining power of customers

- Threat of substitute products or services

"The collective strength of these forces," he writes, "determines the ultimate profit potential of an industry." Owing to these factors, the profit potential will vary from industry to industry. Today, for example, sectors of the telecommunications industry are faced with weak profit potential because so many factors conspire against existing providers: Industry participants are continually fighting to grab their rivals' customers, often by cutting prices and extending services; customers can switch easily; and many communications options are available, including land lines, cell phones, e-mail instant messaging, and Internet phone. Meanwhile, the rapid pace of technological change is forcing the existing players to spend royally to remain on the cutting edge. Participants in other industries, in contrast, may confront a much more favorable combination of the five forces.

The key to growth and survival, according to Porter, is to use one's knowledge of these five forces to "stake out a position that is less vulnerable to attack from head-to-head opponents, whether established or new, and less vulnerable to erosion from the direction of buyers, suppliers, and substitute goods." Such a position, he argues, can be gained by solidifying relationships with profitable customers, product differentiation (either through redesign or marketing), integrating operations, or by gaining technical leadership.[3]

A complete discussion of the five forces framework is beyond the scope of this chapter. Readers are encouraged to obtain the article and apply its concepts to their own industries.

Looking outside for threats and opportunities is one piece of the preparation you must do before you even discuss strategic plans. Great companies do this continually. They send their technical people to professional conferences and subscribe to key academic journals. They are always in touch with current and potential customers via focus groups and interviews with *lead users*—that is, companies and individuals whose needs are far ahead of typical users. Some even set up special "intelligence" units to scan newspapers and technical journals, keep an eye on proposed regulations, and so forth. These companies are constantly sensing the outer world for threats and opportunities that could affect them. Your company should do the same.

Summing Up

- Workstyle and lifestyle trends are likely to affect your future.

- Market segmentation is a useful tool for dividing a large heterogeneous market of customers into smaller segments with homogeneous features. Analysis of these segments can help you understand which are more profitable to serve. Segmentation also makes it easier to identify the met and unmet needs, price sensitivity, accessibility, and loyalty of identifiable customers.

- By determining the price elasticity of demand for your product or service, you can quantify the impact of price changes on customer demand.

- Porter's framework for competitive analysis encourages strategists to examine five industry forces: the threat of new entrants; the threat of substitute products or services; the bargaining power of suppliers; the bargaining power of customers; and tactical jockeying for position among current competitors.

2

SWOT Analysis II

Looking Inside for Strengths and Weaknesses

Key Topics Covered in This Chapter

- *Identifying and assessing core competencies*

- *Understanding your financial capacity for undertaking a new strategy*

- *Evaluating management and organizational culture in terms of change-readiness*

- *A nine-step method for evaluating strengths and weaknesses*

HAVING TESTED THE outer world for threats and opportunities, strategists must look inward and evaluate their strengths and weaknesses as an enterprise. As with the outer world, knowledge of the inner world imparts a practical sense about what company goals and strategies are most feasible and promising.

What are a company or unit's strengths and weaknesses? The cost structure of its operations is one place to look for answers. Another is the company's brands. Are they powerful and capable of extending the organization's reach into the marketplace? How about its pipeline of R&D projects, and the acumen of its employees?

There is much to be considered in an internal analysis. This chapter addresses three of the most important areas in which a company's strengths and weaknesses should be evaluated: core competencies and processes, financial condition, and management and culture. It then presents a method you can use for conducting your evaluations.

Core Competencies

A core competence is a potential foundation for any new or revised strategy. The term *core competency* refers to a company's expertise or skills in key areas that directly produce superior performance. One of Sony's core competencies, for example, is its ability to unite microelectronics and innovative design in a stream of useful consumer products. Corning has enormous competencies in the area of glass and ceramic materials and has used those competencies strategically over the years to produce successful product lines, from Pyrex oven-ware to television tubes to fiber optics to the innards of catalytic converters. Bechtel counts large-scale project management among its core competencies; whether the job is building a new airport for the capital of Peru or a petrochemical complex in China's Guangdong Province, Bechtel know how to tackle a big task and get it done.

What are your company's core competencies? Don't answer this by simply stating what your company does: "We make lighting fixtures." Instead, determine what you are uniquely good at—better than others—and that customers value. In some cases, what you're good at may be a core process—that is, a key activity that turns inputs into outputs. Core processes are the ones that make or break your business. 3M, for example, has a process for turning out dozens of new, customer-pleasing products every year. Over the years, it has learned far better than most how to generate promising ideas—many in the area of adhesives—and convert the best of these into real solutions to consumer and industrial problems. For USAA, the member-owned financial services company, handling customer transactions is a core process, and one that it does particularly well.

One warning. Being exceptionally good at something does not in itself confer a strategic advantage. You must be exceptionally good at something valued by customers. This might seem obvious, but some executives overlook it. You must also be better than others.

One way to assess the relative power of your core competencies and core processes is through *benchmarking*, an objective method for rating one's own activities against similar activities performed by organizations recognized for best practice. In addition to providing a method for rating oneself, benchmarking aims to identify opportunities for process improvement. The benchmark target may very well be in another industry. For example, when Xerox discovered problems in its parts and components logistics operation, it sent a team of people to Freeport, Maine, to study how L.L. Bean, the popular and successful direct-mail clothing and equipment retailer, managed its picking and packing of individual customer orders.

What the Xerox team learned was then used to improve its own handling of customer orders.

Remember, a competency is only meaningful in context. (See "Is Your Unique Competency a Sound Basis for an Effective Strategy?" for a look at evaluating core competencies.)

Here is an example of a method you can use to systematically assess the strength of your core competencies relative to those of rivals. The hypothetical company in this example is Gizmo Products, Inc., a designer and manufacturer of high-end cooking ware. In this exercise, it has compared its competencies in critical areas to those of Company X and Company Y—both serious competitors (see table 2-1). Notice that areas of primary and secondary competitive performance are identified.

Ratings like the ones shown in the table can help managers and executives identify strengths and weaknesses in the areas that matter most. These ratings can often be obtained by means of brainstorming among company personnel. But employee views may lack objectivity and suffer from incomplete knowledge. So, if you adopt this method, be sure to bring in the voices of salespeople, defectors from rival companies, and consultants who know the industry well. Make use of any survey data your market research has conducted on customers and distributors. Also look to quality and repair incidences compiled by objective third parties. What you want is an unvarnished assessment of where your company is strong and weak relative to key competitors.

This method of assessment differs from the traditional benchmarking exercise in that it examines many key aspects of company competence, not just one. And like benchmarking, it has a methodological weakness: It provides a snapshot of where different companies stand at a point in time, when the trajectory of competence is what matters for the future. For example, in table 2-1 Gizmo appears stronger than Company B in terms of flexible manufacturing, a key competency. Gizmo rates a 4 versus Company B's 3 on this important measure. However, Gizmo may be losing relative strength in this area while Company B may be improving rapidly from year to year.

Is Your Unique Competency a Sound Basis for an Effective Strategy?

To be the basis for an effective strategy, a particular core competency or resource must be valued by customers. But it must also pass the following tests, according to David Collis and Cynthia Montgomery:

- **Inimitability.** It must be hard to copy. Don't try to base a long-term strategy on something that your competitors can quickly copy.

- **Durability.** Durability refers to the continuing value of the competence or resource. Some brand names, like Disney's or Coca Cola's, have enduring value. Some technologies, however, have commercial value for only a few years; then they are swept aside by new and better technologies.

- **Appropriability.** This test determines who captures the value created by your competency or unique resource. In some industries, the lion's share of profits goes to retailers, not to the companies whose ingenuity developed and produced the actual products.

- **Sustainability.** Can your special resource by trumped by a substitute?

- **Competitive superiority.** Is your special competence or resource truly superior to those of competitors? As Collis and Montgomery warn, "Perhaps the greatest mistake managers make when evaluating their companies' resources is that they do not assess them relative to competitors'." So always rate your strength against the best of your rivals.

SOURCE: David J. Collis and Cynthia A. Montgomery, "Competing on Resources," *Harvard Business Review* (July–August, 1995), 118–128.

TABLE 2-1

Comparing Core Competencies and Resources

5 = very strong; 1 = very weak

	Gizmo	Company A	Company B
Competencies			
Primary importance			
New product time-to-market	5	2	3
Product quality	4	4	5
Dealer service	4	2	5
Satisfaction of final customers	5	2	4
Developing and attracting human talent	4	2	4
Flexible manufacturing	4	2	3
Secondary importance			
Project management skills	4	?	3
Cost control	4	3	5
IT systems	3	?	4
Critical assets			
Brand power	3	1	4
Supply-chain power	5	1	4
Physical plant	4	2	4
Strategic partnerships	3	2	5
Distribution network	4	3	5

Thus, next year, Gizmo may have lost its lead in flexible manufacturing. So add a sense of trajectory to your assessments, as in table 2-2. This table indicates that Gizmo is declining, Company A is on a plateau, and Company B is improving its competence in flexible manufacturing.

TABLE 2-2

Evaluating Competencies with Trajectory

Arrows indicate the trajectory of relative strength or weakness

	Gizmo	Company A	Company B
Flexible manufacturing	4 ↓	2 →	3 ↑

Financial Condition

If a new strategy is the point of your internal analysis, you'd better assess the current financial strength of your organization. After all, a new strategy may be costly to implement, especially if it potentially involves the purchase of assets or the acquisition of some other operating company or unit. So ask the CFO to provide a full report that includes the following:

- **Cash flows.** To what extent are cash flows from current operations sufficient to support a new initiative? A fast-growing company usually gobbles up cash flow from operations and then has to go hunting for outside capital to finance growth. A mature, low-growth company, in contrast, can often finance a new initiative from operating cash flow from current operations.

- **Access to outside capital.** If cash flow is insufficient to finance a new strategy, the company will have to look to outside creditors and/or investors. So determine the company's (1) borrowing capacity, (2) ability to float bonds at a reasonable rate of interest, and (3) in the event of a major initiative, its ability to attract equity capital through a sale of company stock.

- **Other scheduled capital spending plans.** Your company may have already approved other capital spending projects. If it has, those might absorb all available capital. Get a list of these scheduled projects and determine the extent to which they will compete for resources with any new strategy.

- **Hurdle rate of new projects.** The *hurdle rate* is the minimum rate of return expected from new projects that require substantial capital investments. It is usually calculated as the enterprise's cost of capital plus some expectation of profit.

The financial performance of current operations is also something you should acquire from the CFO—in particular, the company's return on invested capital and its return on assets. You should also know if these return figures are trending upward, trending

downward, or stable. Why bother with these returns? Because they
are measures of profitability, and any new strategy must be capable of
improving on them. These returns represent baselines against which
the contribution of any new strategy must be compared. For example, if the company's current return on invested capital is 12 percent—and stable—any new strategy would have to improve that
measure of profitability.

Management and Culture

Some companies can recognize when a shift in direction is necessary,
and have both the management competence and organizational culture required for successful change. Others do not. It took many
years, for example, for the management of General Motors (GM) to
recognize the seriousness of the threat posed by Asian competitors.
Once those executives were alert to the threat, their well-intended
plans for change were hobbled by a vast organization, installed
plants, and labor contracts that made change difficult and painfully
slow. Employees and critics alike joked that GM stood for "glacial
movement."

Like GM, every established enterprise faces problems of flexibility and adaptability to a greater or lesser extent. Years of practice naturally mold both managerial thinking and organizational forms to
the requirement of the existing strategy. That is a virtue as long as
the strategy makes sense, but a potential handicap when it doesn't.
So, as you look for internal strengths and weaknesses, ask this question: Is the company "change-ready"? A change-ready company is
adaptive and prepared by structure and temperament to discard what
is not working and move to strategies capable of better results. A
change-ready company has these characteristics:

• Managers are respected and effective.

• People feel personally motivated to change.

• The organization is nonhierarchical.

- People are accustomed to collaborative work.

- There is a culture of accountability for results.

- Performance is rewarded.

Companies with these characteristics are in a good position to implement a new strategy. Those that lack them face a stiffer challenge.

A Method for Evaluating Internal Strengths and Weaknesses

While some company strengths and weaknesses can be quantified (e.g., return on assets), many others cannot. Some people may say, "Our company rewards performance," while other employees of the same company may say just the opposite. To cut through these different perceptions, you need a method that involves many perceptive people representing different functions within the organization. Their collective judgment is bound to be more accurate than that of one or two bright individuals who see things from their narrow viewpoints. As James Surowiecki noted in his perceptive book *The Wisdom of Crowds*, "If you put together a big enough and diverse enough group of people and ask them to 'make decisions affecting matters of general interest,' that group's decisions will, over time, be 'intellectually superior to the isolated individual,' no matter how smart or well-informed he is."[1] You also need a method for organizing this collective intelligence, which we offer you here in nine practical steps.[2]

- **Step 1: Select an individual to facilitate the analysis.** This person should be someone whom people trust and respect. He or she should also be viewed as objective and not aligned with any particular camp within the company.

- **Step 2: Create a SWOT team of knowledgeable individuals from different functional areas of the company.** Like the facilitator, team members should be trusted and respected by their peers and have reputations for objectivity and "truth telling."

- **Step 3: Brainstorm the company or unit's strengths.** Go around the room and solicit ideas from everyone. Consider the core competencies, financial condition, and management and organizational culture as described above. Also give some attention to leadership and decision-making abilities, innovation, speed, productivity, quality, service, efficiency, and applied technology processes.

- **Step 4: Record all suggestions on a flip chart.** Avoid duplicate entries. Make it clear that some issues may appear on more than one list. For example, a company or unit may enjoy some strengths in customer service, but have certain weaknesses in that area as well. At this point, the goal is to capture as many ideas on the flip charts as possible. Evaluating these strengths will take place later.

- **Step 5: Consolidate ideas. Post all flip chart pages on a wall.** While every effort may have been taken to avoid duplicate entries, there will be some overlap. Consolidate duplicate points by asking the group which items can be combined under the same heading. Resist the temptation to overconsolidate—lumping lots of ideas under one subject. Often, this results in a lack of focus.

- **Step 6: Clarify ideas.** Go down the consolidated list item by item and clarify any items that participants have questions about. It's helpful to reiterate the meaning of each item before discussing it. Stick to defining strengths. Restrain any urge to talk about solutions at this point in the process.

- **Step 7: Identify the top three strengths.** Sometimes the top three strengths are obvious. In that case, simply test for consensus. Otherwise, give participants a few minutes to pick their top issues and vote on them. Allow each team member to cast three to five votes (three if the list of issues is ten items or fewer, five if it is long). Identify the top three items. If there are ties or the first vote is inconclusive, discuss the highly rated items from the first vote and vote again.

- **Step 8: Summarize company strengths.** Once the top three strengths are decided, summarize them on a single flip chart page.

- **Step 9: Repeat steps 2 through 6 for company or unit weaknesses.** Like strengths, areas of weakness for a company or unit include core competencies, finances, management and culture, leadership abilities, decision-making abilities, speed, innovation, productivity, quality, service, efficiency, and technology.

(Note: You can use this same method in tapping collective insights on threats and opportunities, as described in the preceding chapter on external analysis. You might want to expand the SWOT team, however, to include people from outside the company: a supplier who knows the industry intimately and with whom you work regularly, a consultant with broad industry experience, and so forth.)

Once you have completed the nine steps, your SWOT team should compile its findings in a formal report for the benefit of top management, strategic planners, and other interested parties. And if you've done the same for external analysis, your company will be ready to move on to the business of creating a strategy.

Summing Up

- A core competency is a potential foundation for any new or revised strategy.

- A competency is meaningful only when compared with that of rivals.

- Assess the current financial strength of your organization before thinking about strategy. A new strategy may be costly to implement, especially if it involves the purchase of assets or the acquisition of some other business.

- Management competence and organizational culture are required for successful strategic change.

- Determine if the business is change-ready by looking for these characteristics: Managers are respected and effective; people feel personally motivated to change; the organization is non-hierarchical; people are accustomed to collaborative work; there is a culture of accountability for results; and performance is rewarded.

- Don't rely on one or two people to do internal analysis. Instead, bring together a small group of objective people representing different activities in the organization. Have them use the nine-step process outlined above.

3

Types of Strategy

Which Fits Your Business?

Key Topics Covered in This Chapter

- *Low-cost leadership strategy, and how to make it work*

- *Differentiating a product or service—even a commodity—in ways that create real value for customers*

- *Customer relationship strategy, and six approaches for making it valuable for customers*

- *The network effect strategy: winner-take-all*

- *Determining which strategic approach is right for you*

L OOK AT THE many textbooks on business strategy and you'll find a cornucopia of strategy frameworks: low-cost leadership, diversification, merger-acquisition, global, customer focus, product leadership, vertical integration, flexibility, product/service differentiation, and so forth. What are these strategies? And now that you understand the external environment and your internal strengths and weaknesses, how can you determine which is best and most appropriate for your company?

At bottom, every for-profit entity aims for the same goal: to identify and pursue a strategy that will give it a defensible and profitable hold on some segment of the marketplace. That segment, by choice, may be large or small. It may produce, by choice, high profits on a small number of transactions, or low profits on every one of millions of sales. It may involve superficial relationships with many customers or long-term and deep relationships with just a few. No matter which strategies they follow, these companies will also try to increase the range of profitability—that is, the difference between what customers are willing to pay and the company's cost of providing its goods or services.

This chapter describes four basic strategies: low-cost leadership, product/service differentiation, customer relationship, and network effect. It is difficult to find a business strategy that is not one of these or some variation.

Low-Cost Leadership

Low-cost leadership has paved the road to success for many companies. Discount retailers in the United States such as E.J. Korvette and later Kmart grabbed significant chunks of the retail market away from traditional department stores and specialty stores when they first appeared in the 1950s and 1960s. Their success was a function of their ability to deliver goods at lower prices; and they developed that ability by keeping their cost structures much lower than those of traditional competitors. These early discounters were displaced, in turn, by Wal-Mart and Target, which were even more effective in operating a low-cost strategy.

In this strategy, the product or service is usually the same as the product or service offered by rivals. It may be a commodity, such as rolled steel or household electrical wire, or it may be something readily available through other vendors. Items sold by Wal-Mart, for example, can be obtained at many other locations, some just down the street—Duracell batteries, Minolta binoculars, Canon cameras, Kodak photographic film, Wrangler jeans, Hanes underwear, Gillette razor blades, Bic pens. So why do so many people in North America head to Wal-Mart and Target to buy these items, often driving past rival vendor locations? Because they believe they will get the same items for less money. And they usually do. Wal-Mart in particular was built with this low-cost advantage as a key part of its overall strategy.

The key to success using the low-cost strategy is to deliver the customer's expected level of value at a cost that assures an adequate level of profitability. Consider figure 3-1, which is adapted from a model first advanced by Adam Brandenburger and Harborne Stuart. The vertical distance between the willingness of customers to pay (top line) and the cost of providing the product itself (bottom line) represents the range of pricing within which every company must operate. It also represents the value added by the company, as perceived by customers. For commodity-like or undifferentiated products, the spread between these lines is narrow. And the top line—what customers are willing to pay—is generally fixed. So, to establish

FIGURE 3-1

Expected Value

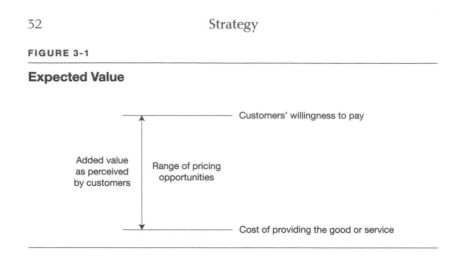

greater profitability, the vendor must push the cost-of-providing line lower. It will generally attempt to do this through operational efficiency, pressuring suppliers for low prices, and other means. This is the game that Wal-Mart has been playing and winning for many years. It has squeezed more costs out of its supply chain than has any other major retailer.

It's easy to assume that the low-cost leadership strategy applies solely to physical products: jeans, paint, tons of steel, and so forth. There are, however, many examples of low-cost strategy in the service sector. Consider The Vanguard Group, a leading investment management company. Started in 1975, the company provides a broad array of mutual funds and a very high level of client service. There is nothing particularly fancy about Vanguard or its funds. While some of its actively managed funds have been top performers over the long term, many are index funds that purposely aim to replicate the return of the market, not "beat" it. In most years, these passive index funds actually outperform the average managed fund.

What really sets Vanguard apart from other fund families is its no-commission policy and the fact that it has the lowest average expense ratio among fund families. In 2003, for example, Vanguard's average expense ratio was a tiny 0.25 percent of assets—less than one-fifth of the mutual fund industry's average expense ratio of 1.38 percent. That has the effect of giving Vanguard clients a 1.13 percent greater annual return on their money (all else being equal). By keeping management and transaction costs low, Vanguard actually invests and reinvests more of a client's money. And that produces better returns over time. Vanguard's success with this strategy has earned it accolades among individual investors and made it one of the largest fund families in the United States.

Making the Low–Cost Strategy Work

As mentioned above, the key to retaining low-cost leadership is keeping the costs of providing goods or services lower than those of competitors. This is a constant challenge, since rivals will be working hard to drive their costs lower than yours. But it can be achieved through several means. Consider these four:

CONTINUOUS IMPROVEMENT IN OPERATING EFFICIENCY. The Japanese developed the philosophy of *kaizen*, or continuous process improvement, to gain their well-known lead in manufacturing. *Kaizen* encourages everyone, from the executive suite to the loading dock, to seek out ways to incrementally improve what they are doing. A 1 percent improvement here and a 2 percent improvement there quickly add up over time, giving the firm a notable cost advantage. The concept of *process reengineering* aims for a similar result, but *kaizen* aims for incremental improvements to the existing work, whereas process engineering aims for large breakthrough change—either through wholesale restructuring or the total elimination of existing activities. Both *kaizen* and process engineering have had profound impacts of operating efficiency in both manufacturing and services.

EXPLOITATION OF THE EXPERIENCE CURVE. Production managers know that people learn to do the same job more quickly and with fewer errors the more frequently they do the job. Thus, a heart operation that once took eight hours to complete can be done successfully in four hours as a surgical team gains more and more experience with the procedure. And before long, they may have it done in two or three hours. The same is observed in manufacturing settings in which managers and employees focus on learning.

The *experience curve* concept holds that the cost of doing a repetitive task decreases by some percentage each time the cumulative volume of production doubles. Thus, a company that gets onto the experience curve sooner than an imitator can theoretically maintain a cost advantage. Consider the two cost curves in figure 3-2. Both companies A and B begin at the same cost level and learn at the same rate. They compete primarily on price. But A got into the business first and, consequently, is further down the cost curve than rival B, maintaining its cost advantage at every point in time. At time T, for instance, that advantage is C. Company B must either learn at a much faster rate, accept a permanent cost disadvantage (and smaller profit margin), or exit the market.

AN UNBEATABLE SUPPLY CHAIN. Everyone is familiar with the Dell business model. It sells its PCs directly to consumers, skipping the middleman. It also builds those PCs to order, thus eliminating the costly finished goods inventory problem that plagues rivals that operate with traditional business models. It has no finished products sitting on the shelf and becoming more and more technically obsolete by the day.

FIGURE 3-2

The Experience Curve

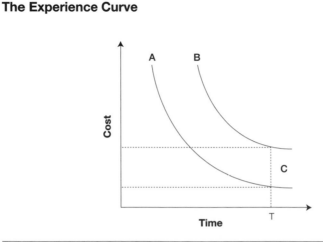

What people often overlook about Dell is the efficiency and effectiveness of its supply chain. That chain includes component suppliers, assemblers, and the logistical services of United Parcel Service. All are digitally linked so that order information can be immediately translated into production and delivery schedules. The ability of this supply chain to deliver a customized PC to a customer's doorstep in a week or so makes it possible to eliminate middlemen and inventory costs, giving the company cost leadership in its field. Wal-Mart provides yet another example of a company that commands cost leadership through the power of its supply chain.

PRODUCT REDESIGN. Huge cost reductions are often achieved through product redesign. For example, back in the 1970s, Black & Decker, a manufacturer of consumer power tools, found itself going head-to-head with low-cost Asian competitors. It had a serious cost disadvantage that could not be cured by simply being more thrifty and efficient. Something more dramatic was required. B&D responded by redesigning its entire family of consumer power tools *and* the process for making them. At the heart of its product line makeover was a single electric motor that could be inexpensively altered to provide power for any number of different hand tools. That eliminated dozens of different motor types as well as the need to make and store hundreds of different components. The core product platform's simplicity and "manufacturability" made it possible to produce the new family of tools with 85 percent lower labor costs. Inventory and other related costs tumbled by similar percentages. The Société Micromécanique et Horlogère (Swiss Corporation for Microelectronics and Watchmaking Industries Ltd.) accomplished similar results with its development of the Swatch watch, which was based on the company's development of a reliable, plastic, quartz timekeeper that could be mass-produced for a tiny fraction of the cost of traditional watchworks. This design breakthrough made it possible for the Swiss company to compete and prosper in a market dominated by low-cost Asian competitors.

In these and other cases, product redesign proved to be an effective tool for achieving cost leadership.

. . .

Operational excellence is an important part of low-cost leadership strategy, but only a part. As we'll see later, becoming the low-cost leader involves more than pinching pennies and squeezing the fat out of business processes. Above all it entails a thoughtful plan for structuring the enterprise. Consider this analogy: If you want to be the fastest sailboat in your area, you don't simply wax the hull and train your crew to get the most out of the floating bathtub you call your boat—instead, you build a craft that is designed for speed from the keel up. The business equivalent is to structure the organization to deliver low-cost leadership.

Is a low-cost strategy feasible for your company? If it is, what would have to happen to make it work?

Differentiation

Every successful strategy is about *differentiation*, even the low-cost leadership strategy. "We can fly you to Genoa for less than our competitors." "At Auto City Sales, we will not be undersold." But for most companies, differentiation is expressed in some qualitative way that customers value. For example, when Thomas Edison first began to market his system of electric incandescent lighting, his principal rivals were local gas companies. Both methods of illumination were effective, but Edison's approach had clear differences that most customers favored. Unlike gas lamps, electric lighting didn't noticeably heat up people's living rooms on hot summer nights. It was more convenient, requiring just a flick of the switch to turn it on and off. And it eliminated a serious fire hazard in many applications. Edison played on these qualitative differences as he attacked and eliminated the gas companies' dominance of urban lighting in the late 1800s.

Companies today likewise adopt *differentiation strategies*. Consider the auto industry. Volvo touts the crashworthiness of its vehicles to set itself apart. Toyota plays on its reputation for quality and high resale value; more recently it has differentiated its Prius model with hybrid engine technology. The Mini Cooper practically screams "I'm fun to drive" to potential buyers. Porsche has also differentiated itself by concentrating on the development of high-performance sports cars—while GM may offer a vehicle for every household budget, and Toyota may claim a high level of quality and reliability, neither have much appeal for the small number of drivers who look for speed, agility, and a sense that they could handle the raceway circuit at LeMans. That is what Porsche aims to deliver through its strategy of differentiation.

Differentiating a Commodity Product

Even among commodity products, business strategists have found and exploited opportunities to differentiate themselves. Although price and product features may be identical, it is still possible to differentiate on the basis of service. The cement business provides an example. Cement is cement, right? That's the fact Mexico-based CEMEX, the world's third-largest provider of cement, is faced with. Cement is a commodity product. Nevertheless, CEMEX has developed a strategy of fast and reliable delivery that qualitatively differentiates the company from its many rivals. As described by David Bovet and Joseph Martha in their book on supply-chain excellence, CEMEX has become a major industry power in many markets because it adopted a production and high-tech logistics strategy that achieves on-time delivery 98 percent of the time, versus the 34 percent record of most competitors. For construction companies operating on tight schedules, that reliability is highly valued, especially when a late delivery means that dozens of highly paid crew members will be standing around doing nothing. "This super reliability" write Bovet and Martha, "allows [CEMEX] to charge a premium in most markets, contributing to profit levels 50 percent higher than those of its key competitors."[1] In this case, super reliability has effectively differentiated a commodity product. Something similar may be achieved by offering superior customer support.

Effective Differentiation

Is your company following a strategy of differentiation? If it is, what sets it apart from the products and services of rivals? Whatever the answer, remember that differentiation only matters to the extent that *customers value the difference*. Maybe not all customers, but the ones you have targeted. If these customers truly value that which sets your product or service apart, they will either (1) select your offering over those of others, (2) be willing to pay a premium for what you offer, or (3) act on some combination of 1 and 2. Experience and market research are the best ways to determine if your difference will be valued by customers.

Customer Relationship

Everyone knows that you can buy a camera or wide-angle lens for less at Wal-Mart, Best Buy, or one of the other discount stores. Film and film-processing are cheaper at these stores as well. But many people still patronize small, independently owned photography shops when they purchase cameras, accessories, and films. Likewise, Fantastic Sams, a national franchise, provides great hairstyling services at low prices, yet many—if not most—women will pay more to go to the stylist who has been handling their hair for the past many years. Many women, in fact, can claim a longer-term relationship with their male hairstylists than with their husbands! In the words of one, "A husband is replaceable—a good hairdresser isn't."

What's going on here? Why do so many customers pay more to patronize local camera shops, hairdressers, corner bookstores, neighborhood meat markets and bakeries, and many other vendors of goods and services when they could get a cheaper deal elsewhere? The reason is that they *value* the personal relationship experienced in doing business with these companies, their owners, and their employees. That relationship can take many forms: doing business with a familiar face; the fact that the vendor knows the customers and their needs; or the vendor's willingness to explain the product, how to use it, and the pros and cons of different purchase choices. These are qualities you cannot find online, in a direct-mail catalog, or at most "big-box" stores. Those vendors provide a transaction, but not a relationship.

Relationship Strategy at Work: USAA

While big companies are at a disadvantage in building and executing a customer relationship strategy, it is not impossible. (See "Focus Strategy—What's Different?" for another way of creating a a good customer experience.) Consider the case of USAA (United States Automobile Association). Not many readers will have ever heard of this *Fortune* 500 financial services company even though it has $71 billion under management. That's because it caters exclusively to a very small slice of the total U.S. population: active duty officers and enlisted personnel, National Guard and Reserve officers and enlisted personnel, officer candidates, as well as dependents and former spouses of the above.

The people in USAA's target market, however, know the company very well, and a large percentage of them are customers of its banking, insurance, and credit card services. Among active-duty officers, participation is 90 to 95 percent. And because it is a mutual company, customers are also part-owners.

After decades of serving this population, USAA understands its unique banking, insurance, and retirement needs. And it knows how to deal with the fact that military officers are transferred from post to post and around the world with great frequency. Its understanding of customers is expressed in many ways that people appreciate. For example, when customers are deployed overseas or to a war zone, their cars are usually put in storage for one or more years; in these cases USAA urges them to request elimination of the costly liability component of their auto insurance policies. No other auto insurer would think to do that. And unlike other life insurers, its policies have no war clause provision. USAA customers know that full policy death benefits will be paid if they die for *any* reason, including wartime service.

USAA's close relationship with its military clientele and its understanding of their unique lifestyle can be traced back to its founding in 1922 by twenty-five army officers who found it difficult—owing to their profession and mobility—to obtain auto insurance. Even today, a substantial number of USAA executives and employees are former military people, and customer-serving employees are given extensive

Focus Strategy—What's Different?

Many authors point to focus as one of the generic strategies. As described by Michael Porter in his landmark book, a *focus strategy* is one that is "built around serving a particular target very well, and each functional policy is developed with this in mind."[a] In many respects the focus strategy and customer relationship strategy go hand-in-hand. It is next to impossible to develop serious relationships with anything but a highly focused, clearly targeted customer segment, as in the USAA example. On the other hand, a focus strategy can exist independent of relationships. Consider the case of Cracker Barrel Old Country Store, a nationwide chain of restaurant/gift shops that focuses on travelers who like traditional foods, particularly motorists who travel the U.S. interstate highway system. Cracker Barrel offers country-style meals and gift items in each of its locations. To encourage repeat visits, the company Web site includes a "trip planner" that identifies the locations of all Cracker Barrel outlets along any "to-from" driving route. It is doubtful that many travelers perceive any relationship benefits from their visits to Cracker Barrel, but they do seem to appreciate the consistency of the food, ambience, and shopping opportunities it provides. Repeat customers know exactly what to expect from these facilities, which makes the choice of where to stop for a meal easy for people on long driving trips.

[a] Michael E. Porter, *Competitive Strategy* (New York: The Free Press, 1980), 38.

training on the unique financial needs of military personnel.[2] Personal service is their highest priority.

USAA focuses on a much narrower market segment than just about any other *Fortune* 500 company, but that focus and attention to customer relationships has paid off in terms of revenue growth, profitability, and customer satisfaction. In 2004, a poll of affluent investors put USAA at the top, with a satisfaction score 8 percent higher than TIAA-CREF, which also serves a highly focused market group, and 73 percent higher than Fidelity, which serves the general public. That same year, a survey conducted by Forrester Research put the company at the top among financial services companies for customer advocacy. Customer advocacy, according to that study, is customers' perception that a company is doing what's best for them and not just for the company's profitability. "USAA scored highest in our ranking, in part," according to a Forrester news release, "because of its focus on simplifying customers' lives through efficient call center experiences. Many large banks, on the other hand, are at the bottom of our ranking because many of their customers feel nickel-and-dimed."[3]

Making the Customer Relationship Strategy Work

Companies like USAA succeed to the extent that the relationships they build with people add real value—as perceived by customers. That value can take many forms:

- **Simplifying customers' lives or work.** A USAA auto insurance holder does not have to obtain a new insurance policy every time he or she is transferred to another state.

- **Ongoing benefits.** Microsoft gains relationship points through its practice of notifying software users of critical updates, which can be downloaded by customers without charge.

- **Personalized service.** Many top-tier hotels have developed personalized approaches to handling repeat visitors by storing check-in information and customer preferences in their companywide data bases. This enables express check-in, gives customers the service they want, and adds a personal touch: "Welcome back to XYZ Hotels, Mr. Jones. We have a non-smoking room for you. Do you still prefer having the *Wall Street Journal* delivered with your continental breakfast?"

- **Customized solutions.** Most companies continue to sell one-size-fits-all products and service; if you can develop the ability to economically customize your offering to the unique requirements of individual customers, you will build a stronger personal connection to them.

- **Personal contact.** Instead of channeling incoming customer calls to whichever service rep is available, give every established customer an account representative; this puts a personal voice on what would otherwise be an impersonal transaction.

- **Continuous learning.** Many companies have adopted CRM (customer relationship management) techniques to better understand and serve their most loyal and profitable customers. CRM identifies contact points between customer and company, and views each as an opportunity to learn more about customer needs.

A strategy based on customer relationships can produce powerful results and strong customer loyalty. The danger, of course, is that many people profess a strong affinity for the personal touch but turn to the low-cost provider when large sums are at stake. As one homeowner put it, "I usually patronize the small hardware store in my neighborhood. The owner knows me and I can count on him for advice when I have to repair a leaky faucet, install ceramic tile, or do some other job. But when it comes to big purchases—expensive power tools or something of that nature—I end up at Home Depot. I can't afford not to." The vendor's challenge in these cases is to keep control of major purchases.

Network Effect Strategy

When the first telephones were sold in the late nineteenth century, they weren't particularly useful. A person could only call one of the few other owners of the new gadget. But the telephone's utility grew as more and more homes, stores, and offices joined the telephone network. This is called the *network effect*—a phenomenon in which the value of a product increases as more products are sold and the network of users increases.

As a strategy, the network effect is fairly new. Perhaps its most obvious practitioner and beneficiary is eBay, the online auction company. eBay began as a hobby business of its founder, Pierre Omidyar, who developed software and an online system that allowed individuals to list new and used items of all types for auction. His wasn't the first online auction site, but it was the first to become widely popular, and that popularity sent the network effect into high gear. Buyers flocked to eBay over other sites because it had the most sellers, and sellers listed their items on eBay because it attracted the most buyers. This virtuous circle quickly established Omidyar's site as the dominant online auction site, and it continues to support eBay's remarkable growth.

There is no evidence that Omidyar and his colleagues set out with an implicit network effect strategy. It simply happened. However, early success encouraged them to use their rising tide of revenue to keep the ball rolling, which they did through heavy investments in site development, customer service, brand recognition, and a number of strategic acquisitions.

Success with a network strategy depends heavily on a company's ability to get out in front and become the dominant provider. Doing so leaves very little space available for challengers, which is why some call this a *winner-take-all strategy*. eBay quickly dominated its industry. Microsoft did the same with its Windows operating system, though most experienced computer users agree that the user-friendly Macintosh operating system developed by Apple Computer is superior to Windows. But Apple kept its operating system proprietary, while Microsoft allowed its operating system to be installed on all PC manufacturers' machines. Thus, since most PCs operated with Windows, most new software was developed for Windows machines. And because most software was Windows-based, more people bought PCs equipped with the Windows operating system. To date, no one has broken this virtuous circle.

This chapter has presented four general strategies. Each has been a winning ticket for any number of companies. Chances are that one or another—or some variation—would be appropriate for your company. But which one? Look for the answer in your company's mission, its goals, and what you have managed to learn through external and internal analysis, as described in figure 3-3. Think of the mission as setting the boundaries within which you may seek a new strategy. Your goals set the bar of achievement that the strategy must be capable of attaining. Then use SWOT analysis to identify threats and opportunities as well as the current capabilities of the organization. These three factors—in consultation with people who know and understand the many facets of your industry—will guide you to the right choice.

You should understand, however, that any strategic choice involves trade-offs. If you choose to focus on a narrow set of customers, as in the USAA example, you'll have to give up the idea of serving the broad general market. As Michael Porter has warned, "Companies that try to be all things to all customers . . . risk confusion in the trenches as employees attempt to make day-to-day operating decisions without a clear framework."[4] Thus, if you want to be the low-cost retailer in your field, don't try to set up a special boutique chain of stores to cater to high-end customers. You'll confuse the market and yourself—and probably lose lots of money.

FIGURE 3-3

Which Strategy Is Best?

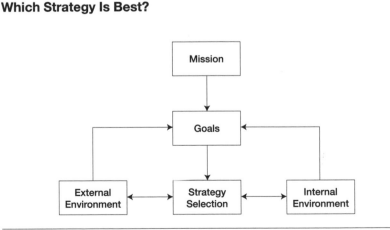

Above all, make sure that your choice of strategy is aligned with the primary customer market you plan to address. This may be the most critical factor in strategy creation. Keep your chosen customer market in your sights at all times, and make sure that your colleagues do the same. Alignment between strategy and customers is absolutely essential.

Summing Up

- As a strategy, low-cost leadership is most appropriate in industries in which competitors essentially offer a commodity-like product or service.

- Continuous improvement in operating efficiency, process reengineering, exploitation of the experience curve, supply-chain power, and product redesign are among the methods used to achieve low-cost leadership.

- A differentiation strategy sets the product or service apart from those of rivals in a qualitative way.

- Commodity products—those with standard features, quality, and price—can be differentiated from those of rivals by means of faster, more reliable delivery and/or superior customer support.

- Strong customer relationships can be used to retain customers who would otherwise gravitate toward lower-cost providers.

- To be effective, a customer relationship strategy must provide something that customers value—for example, something that simplifies their lives or work, ongoing benefits, personalized service, or customized solutions.

- The network effect is a phenomenon in which the value of a product increases as more products are sold. Companies that pursue this strategy (or benefit from it) succeed to the extent that they can get out in front and become the dominant provider of some enabling product or service, such as eBay's online auction site or Microsoft's Windows operating system.

• Whichever strategy type you consider, always look for alignment between the strategy and your target customer market.

4

Strategic Moves

The Mechanisms of Success

Key Topics Covered in this Chapter

- *Gaining a beachhead in occupied terrain*

- *Using innovation to overcome barriers to entry*

- *Applying the principles of judo strategy*

- *Gaining market entry through product differentiation*

- *Creating and then dominating a new market*

- *Bypassing entry barriers through acquisition*

THE PREVIOUS CHAPTER identified the most common strategy types: low-cost leadership; product/service differentiation; customer relationship (and focus); and network effect. There's much more to strategy than deciding which version or variant of these strategies is best for your company. This chapter continues the discussion, indicating how strategy can be used to enter and build defensible positions in the marketplace. It explores a number of potential strategic moves. The discussion here is selective owing to the "essentials" nature of this book. But they should get you thinking about what your company might accomplish.

Gaining a Market Beachhead

In his classic book on military strategy, *On War*, Carl von Clausewitz told his nineteenth-century readers that "Where absolute superiority is not attainable, you must produce a relative one at the decisive point by making skillful use of what you have." Von Clausewitz's advice reminds us that the strategist must reckon with the realities of the market and the existence of competing firms, some of which will have greater market power and financial resources.[1] This means that one must strike in an area of competitor weakness or where the competitor is unlikely to fight back, or will fail to fight back effectively. The strategy chosen, then, must be made in view of this situation.

Consider the case of the U.S. auto industry during the 1960s and 1970s. None of the domestic automakers of the time were skilled at producing small, fuel-efficient vehicles. This was not the result of engineering ineptitude; there simply wasn't strong demand for small cars in the United States. Fuel prices relative to incomes were very low, and most consumers liked roomier vehicles. Also, profits on the few small cars made or sold in America—both in terms of margin and absolute dollars—were far lower than those obtained from larger vehicles. Detroit automakers said "Why bother?" to small cars. Nevertheless, a small segment of market gravitated to small, affordable, fuel-efficient cars. The VW Beetle had already become something of a statement among students, the thrifty, and antiestablishment types.

Before long, Datsun, Fiat, and Renault had joined VW in bringing their small, economical vehicles to the low end of the huge U.S. market, where they had, in Clausewitzian terms, relative superiority, and where they were largely unopposed by domestic producers. Toyota, Mitsubishi, Honda, and others followed and successfully established themselves. The fuel shortages and price spikes of the 1970s gave these small-car makers a huge boost and positioned them to move upstream into larger, more profitable segments. Figure 4-1 indicates how foreign producers, particularly from Asia, moved

FIGURE 4-1

Moving Beyond the Beachhead

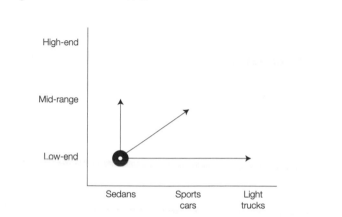

strategically from their initial beachheads into different market segments, mostly into the mid-range. By the 1990s, some of these producers were introducing cars like the Lexus to challenge the high-end, profit-rich sedan segment; and they did the same in the fast-growing light-truck category.

Asian watchmakers followed a similar approach in the early 1970s when they entered the low end of the personal timekeeper market, where unit sales were potentially large but profits were small, and opposition from the dominant companies was weak. Precision watchmakers were unwilling to contest the Asian companies in those low-margin markets, but were content to retreat into the upper-end, high-profit segments of the market. Once the newcomers had established a beachhead, however, they developed products for those high-profit segments as well, forcing established European and North American producers to either compete more intensely or fold.

The lesson in both these examples is to follow Clausewitz's timeless advice of aiming the sharp end of the spear where rivals are weak or uninterested in what you're doing. That advice is applicable in just about every industry. Sam Walton, for example, did not initially go head-to-head with Sears or J.C. Penney, the retail giants of his day. Instead, he located his new Wal-Mart stores in small towns that were not served by those formidable rivals.

Think for a moment about the segments in your industry. Draw a map similar to figure 4-1. Which are the undefended segments where you could establish a beachhead? Once a beachhead is established, what would it take to expand into more profitable adjacent segments?

Market Entry Through Process Innovation

Some entry barriers cannot be outflanked as described above; they must be confronted directly. Doing so can be costly and dangerous if one plays the same game as the established competitors, and is likely to weaken both attacker and defender. The better approach is to bring an innovation to the market—something that will turn the strengths of entrenched rivals into weaknesses.

For example, when Nucor Corporation first began thinking about entering the rolled-steel market, it faced huge, entrenched rivals that had already invested billions in the enormous plants needed to produce rolled steel at competitive rates. Nucor couldn't make those investments and still make money. Its solution was to develop an entirely new, more cost-effective approach to manufacturing the same product. More specifically, it licensed an unproven German technology for "continuous casting," the Holy Grail of steelmakers for over one hundred years, and made that technology work. Next, it decided to use scrap steel as its raw material. The big producers were vertically integrated; they dug raw iron ore from the earth, then shipped it to blast furnaces where mattress-sized blocks of steel were poured and formed. These blocks, in turn, were run through miles of milling machines and reheating furnaces that gradually reduced them to long, thin ribbons of steel. Nucor skipped all those highly capitalized and labor-intensive steps in favor of an electric furnace that could melt scrap into molten steel on the spot as needed.

In the end, newcomer Nucor was able to produce the same quality steel at a lower cost through the power of process innovation. That edge made Nucor both successful and profitable. Thanks to its innovative "mini-mills," it has become the largest U.S. steel producer and is consistently profitable in an industry plagued by wide swings in customer demand. Its return on invested capital is a stunning 25 percent. "Big Steel," in contrast, discovered that its strengths—huge plants and labor forces, mining operations, and so forth—were now weaknesses.

Nucor is not alone among companies that have used process innovation to successfully enter the turf of bigger, more established rivals. Nor is its strategy reserved for small upstarts. Pilkington Glass, for example, became the dominant player in the plate-glass industry through the successful development of the "float glass" process. Like Nucor, it found a method for continual casting that reduced manufacturing time and costs by orders of magnitude.

Whether yours is a product or service company, process innovation may be your ticket to entering or gaining dominance in your target market. Have you or anyone else in your company given this approach any thought?

Applying Judo Strategy

Judo masters use principles of movement, balance, and leverage to defeat more powerful opponents. David Yoffie and Mary Kwak have incorporated these principles into what they term *judo strategy.* They argue that businesspeople can use these principles as they confront larger and stronger competitors. As they tell their readers, "Movement throws your competitors off balance and neutralizes their initial advantages. Balance helps you engage with the competition and survive an attack. And leverage can enable you to bring your opponents down. When used together, these three principles will help you defeat rivals of any size."[2] Here are a few examples of Yoffie and Kwak's three principles at work:

Principle 1: Movement

This principle encourages the strategist to avoid actions, such as a direct challenge, that would invite an attack from more powerful rivals. Capital One employed what Yaffie and Kwak describes as the "Puppy Dog Ploy," avoiding attack by developing its business in ways that didn't bring unwanted attention to itself. For example, when the company rolled out a new offer to another segment of the credit card market, it didn't advertise the offer or talk to the press about its plans. It simply sent out thousands of direct mail pieces to targeted prospects. Even if they intercepted a number of those pieces, Citibank and other large competitors had no way of knowing Capital One's intention.

The movement principle also directs strategists to address opportunities to which muscle-bound and slower-moving opponents are unable to respond. Large firms, like Big Steel in the Nucor case, have amassed substantial physical assets, production methods, labor contracts, and customer relationships. These assets make change difficult. They cannot simply walk away from them. They lack flexibility. Small, newcomer firms lack the muscle of these larger competitors, but can usually move more nimbly to address new market opportunities and adopt new processes. In this sense they avoid head-on confrontation with powerful rivals.

Principle 2: Balance

Success through movement will eventually bring a firm into a confrontation with a larger opponent. In these cases, Yoffie and Kwak recommend avoiding a situation in which you simply trade punches. That's a loser's game for the less powerful firm. When attacked, their judo advice is "push when pulled," using the attacker's own strength to advance your position.

They give the example of Drypers, which was trying hard to establish itself as a maker of infant diapers. The industry goliath, Procter & Gamble, had blanketed Texas with coupons to squelch Drypers' introduction in that important market. "Unable to match P&G's promotional campaign . . . Drypers just accepted its rival's coupons. The more coupons P&G distributed, the more diapers Drypers sold."[3] In effect, Drypers became the beneficiary of its rival's costly promotion program.

Principle 3: Leverage

According to Yoffie and Kwak, the judo strategist applies leverage by turning its opponent's strengths into weaknesses. This can be accomplished by creating conflict between a competitor and its allies—causing them to fight among themselves instead of fighting with you. It can also be accomplished by doing something that transforms the rival's assets into handicaps. They give the example of Freeserve, the leading U.K. Internet service provider, which was faced with dire competition from AOL. AOL had invested heavily in brand, content, and customer service. Using a very different business model, Freeserve was able to offer—as the name states—free Internet access. "[This move] forced AOL to make a painful decision: whether to match Freeserve, thereby killing its high-margin, high-cost core business, or stick to its strategy and see its market share fall."[4]

. . .

Are the principles of judo strategy appropriate for you? If you're small and new, or if you're moving into territory dominated by a powerful rival, they can probably help. But before you try, learn the details of the principles and application tactics of the authors' book.

Market Entry Through Product Differentiation

Product differentiation is another strategy for gaining a market foothold. Inventor Edwin Land and the company he founded, Polaroid, did this in the photographic imaging business. During the 1950s, when Land was developing his technology, the photography business was already mature. Kodak dominated that business and many of its niches. Land would never make headway by producing his own brand of traditional films and cameras; that market was already well served. So he differentiated his product, creating a film capable of developing itself in one minute. This was new. This was different. And it set Polaroid's products apart. Instant photography was a big hit with many consumers, so much so that it allowed Land's company to flourish for several decades.

To be successful, product differentiation must be valued by targeted customers. That's fairly obvious. But it must also be protected by patents or proprietary methods that make its duplication by rivals difficult or impossible. This is an aspect of differentiation that many overlook. George Eastman, founder of Kodak, hit the mother lode with his innovation of photographic film on a roll of cellulose. But Eastman went a step further. Understanding how easily his product could be duplicated by others, he protected it and the equipment developed to manufacture it with an impenetrable thicket of patents. That protection helped his company stake out and dominate the photographic film business for generations.

Eastman's level of success is difficult to replicate. Most product differentiators are lucky if they can capture more than a two- or three-year monopoly. Consider the experience of Minnetonka Corporation, a small, Minnesota-based firm that introduced a product called "Soft Soap" to a mature market dominated by huge national corporations. Soft Soap came in a small plastic bottle with a handy pump. Liquid hand soap isn't rocket science. Anyone with a small laboratory and rudimentary knowledge of chemistry could develop a marketable version of it. In fact, the first liquid soap developed in the United States received its patent in 1865. Over a century later, in 1980, Minnetonka introduced and branded its own version, which was a big hit. Any one of the big soap producer-distributors—companies that controlled shelf space in retail stores across the continent—could have introduced a rival version and smothered the upstart innovator under a tidal wave of promotion and store incentives. But Minnetonka had taken steps to protect itself in the short term by buying up the entire supply of plastic pumps needed for the liquid soap dispensers. That held the competition at bay for a while. Eventually, in 1987, Minnetonka Corporation sold its liquid soap business to the Colgate Company, which has extended the brand with many product variations.

Create and Dominate a New Market

Are you struggling to match or outperform your rivals on cost, quality, or features? That might be a loser's game. A better approach might be to invent an entirely new market where no competitor has yet ventured. (See "Breaking Free of the Old Formula.") And if you blanket key niches of that new market with good products or services, you will achieve a level of dominance that raises high entry barriers to others.

Consider Sony, which conceived of the personal portable stereo market and a product for tapping it: the Walkman. First introduced in 1979, the Walkman gave consumers great sound at a low price, in a small package that could be carried in a coat pocket or briefcase, or attached to a jogger's waistband. No boom box could rival it. Millions of commuters, music buffs, joggers, and people stuck in office cubicles from nine to five bought them. To fill the many segments of

Breaking Free of the Old Formula

Success is often a barrier to market innovation because it enforces a formula that hamstrings innovation and change. For example, back in the late 1970s, the computing world was dominated by powerful mainframe computers, and IBM dominated that business. So, when personal computers began to appear, there wasn't a lot of interest within IBM. The people with organizational clout and big budgets were mainframers who understood the making of big computers and their distribution via corporate leases. Desktop computing and the selling of small, inexpensive machines to individuals were alien ideas within IBM. The only way the company could get its first PC into the market was through a *skunk works* of engineers it set up in Boca Raton, Florida, far from the company's center of power.

Sometimes the best approach to breaking free of the old formula and addressing a new market is through a new subsidiary or new operating unit that has been given substantial autonomy—and no rule book.

this new market, and thereby achieve dominance, Sony introduced different versions of the Walkman, almost all based on the same product platform: a more rugged sports version, one that included AM/FM radio, and so forth. And though rivals soon entered the market with versions of their own, Sony remained dominant and continued to introduce new models.

What Sony accomplished decades ago has today been leapfrogged by the Apple iPod, a pocket-sized digital sound system capable of storing thousands of music files. These are fast becoming a "must-have" item for music lovers of all persuasions. Between its market launch in October 2001 and late 2004, consumers snapped up 5.7 million units. "It's one of the most in-demand electronics gift for the holidays," declared a spokesperson for Best Buy, a major electronics retailer, in December of 2004.

Like Sony before it, Apple has begun offering iPod variants for different market segments, all based on the basic product platform. As of late 2004, these included iPod Photo, a device capable of storing thousand of photo *and* music files, and the special edition iPod U2, which comes preloaded with every tune recorded by that popular rock group. The low-priced iPod "Mini" was launched in early 2005 with great success.

To create a new market, shift your thinking from building and making products to something more basic: satisfying customer's most pressing needs in new ways. Ask, "What could we offer customers if we forgot everything we know about our industry's current rules and traditions? How might we combine the advantages of several industries' offerings to provide new value for buyers?"

Throwing away the rule book and starting with a clean slate isn't easy—especially if you've been successful under those rules—but it's the only way to think your way to new, competition-free markets.

Buying Your Way In

Sometimes the quickest and surest way of entering a new market or expanding substantially in an existing one is to buy your way in by means of a strategic acquisition, merger, or joint venture partnership. Consider this example:

A U.K.-based manufacturer recognized several industrialized Asian countries as expansion opportunities. It had sent people from London to Japan, South Korea, and China to open up sales offices, but all had come back empty-handed. It then tried to set up sales and distribution agreements with local companies, but these initiatives, too, produced no results. Eventually, it decided that the most fruitful approach would be to form a new company with an Asian partner. That partner knew the market, had an established distribution network, and understood the cultural requirements for business success in the target market. Under the terms of the joint venture, the U.K. company would provide two-thirds of the required capital and ship its goods to a warehouse owned by the partners in Hong Kong. The Asian partner would distribute those goods along with its own products, and be credited for every U.K. product sale. It, in turn, would ship some of its Asian-made products to the U.K. partner, which would distribute them on a best-effort basis, taking a cut of all sales.

A joint venture arrangement is just one of many approaches to breaking into a market. Each brings something the other needs to the venture, and each aims to extract a share of the benefits. As a means of entering an unfamiliar market, it is almost always faster than going it alone. It also provides learning opportunities for the partners.

Another approach is to simply buy a company that makes a product or serves a market that fits your strategic plan. Fleet Bank expanded its operations in the northeastern United States during the 1990s and the opening years of the new century through an aggressive strategy of acquisitions. It was in turn gobbled up by Charlotte, North Carolina–based Bank of America, which had the same goal. On a different front, eBay acquired the live auction house Butterfield & Butterfield as part of its strategy of rapidly consolidating as much of the auction "space" as possible. It then bought Kruse International, a leading vendor of collector-quality automobiles, for that same purpose.

Strategists in these cases face the classic build-versus-buy decision. And maybe you do too.

Buying may be the fastest route to your goal, but success is by no means assured. In fact, most research on acquisitions indicates a very high level of disappointment, if not outright failure. In the course of research for his book *Good to Great*, author Jim Collins asked one of his associates to determine the role of large mergers and acquisitions in creating exceptional result. As Collins described to readers of his column in *Time*, ". . . while you can buy your way to growth, you cannot buy your way to greatness." Worse, "Two big mediocrities joined together never make one great company." While mediocre companies made no headway in seeking greatness through M&A activities, good companies (in Collins's definition) found that their best acquisitions met three litmus tests: (1) the acquisition accentuated what the company did better than all other companies; (2) the acquisition enhanced a powerful pre-existing economic engine; and (3) the acquisition "fit the driving passions of the company's people."[5]

This chapter has described a handful of practical approaches to entering markets. Perhaps one will apply to your situation. The total universe of these approaches is limited only by the human imagination. Be aware, however, that one's range of strategic possibilities is generally limited by practical constraints. For example, as described above, Sony and Apple successfully created new markets and filled key niches with imaginative products, but few business organizations have the creative talent, customer knowledge, financial capital, and technical wherewithal to do the same. Likewise, a market-entry strategy based on a joint venture assumes that the instigator has something special to offer the venture partner. Not every firm has that.

So consider the strategic moves described here, but think also about your ability to adopt any one of them. What are the constraints on your ability to make a strategic move? What could be done to relax those constraints?

Summing Up

- Gaining and securing a market beachhead—even in a low-end or low-margin segment—can put you in a position to eventually expand into more attractive and profitable segments.

- When barriers to market entry are dauntingly high, avoid a costly direct assault. Instead, try to develop a new and superior process for doing what entrenched rivals are now doing.

- Judo strategy, as conceptualized by David Yoffie and Mary Kwak, is based on three principles: movement, balance, and leverage. Each is useful when competing with larger stronger businesses.

- To be successful, product differentiation must be valued by targeted customers. To provide a defensible position, it must also be protected by patents or proprietary methods that make its duplication by rivals difficult or impossible.

- Acquisitions and joint ventures offer other strategic moves to entering or expanding within a market. But beware—they often result in disappointment or failure.

5

From Strategy to Implementation

Seeking Alignment

Key Topics Covered in This Chapter

- *The profound differences between strategy creation and strategy implementation*

- *Alignment for implementation*

- *The elements of successful implementation: people, incentives, supportive activities, organizational structure, culture, and leadership*

MANY EXECUTIVES ENJOY strategizing. SWOT analysis involves lots of hard work, but once that's done, these executives can play the part of the armchair general, develop bold initiatives to outflank rivals, corral customers, and conquer markets. Strategy, however, is nothing but hot air if equal or greater attention is not given to the harder and less glamorous work of implementation. *Implementation* describes the concrete measures that translate strategic intent into actions that produce results. Implementation requires continuous managerial attention at all levels. Unlike strategy creation, which is entrepreneurial and market-oriented, implementation is operations-oriented. Implementation excellence is both absolutely essential and capable of providing enormous rewards. (See "Two Very Different Activities" for characteristics that define strategy versus implementation.)

Consider the case of Herman Miller, Inc. The Michigan-based company is a leader in the North American office-furniture industry and a vendor to major corporations. In the early 1990s its leadership recognized that small businesses represented a fast-growing and underserved market. Unlike deep-pocketed corporate clients, these small enterprises watched every penny and had short planning cycles; they were less interested in Miller's countless feature choices for workstations, desks, chairs, and fabrics than in office furnishings that were relatively inexpensive and delivered quickly and on time.[1]

Two Very Different Activities

The differences between strategy creation and strategy implementation are profound. Even the vocabulary used to describe them is very different.

Strategy Creation	Implementation
Analysis and planning	Execution
Thinking	Doing
Initiate	Follow through
At the top	Top-to-bottom
Entrepreneurial	Operational
Goal-setting	Goal-achieving

Herman Miller's management responded in 1995 with a new strategy that aimed to provide these smaller customers with a limited range of basic, mass-customized office furniture that fit these requirements. This was a great strategy for addressing a growing market segment, but more than good intentions were needed to make the strategy successful. Operations within Herman Miller had to change. It couldn't simply throw orders from its small business customers into its existing fulfillment machinery and expect it to deliver what had been promised. But what had to be done?

Company managers approached the implementation problem by first standing back and looking at its current key processes, from order taking to order filling to delivering and installing finished products. Based on that analysis, they energized a lean new operating unit, which they called SQA (for simple, quick, affordable). They also created a new supply chain for SQA capable of delivering on their promise to customers. All participants in that chain, including outside vendors, were linked through a new, state-of-the-art information system that assured both speed and accuracy. Managers and supervisors then went to work, making sure that everyone from the sales staff to assembly personnel to delivery and installation employees understood the importance of being fast, error-free, and on time.

Herman Miller's efforts produced exceptional results. Once implementation was complete and fine-tuned through practice, SQA had collapsed the normal order-to-delivery cycle from the six-to-eight-week industry average to two weeks or less. On-time error-free delivery, which Miller's traditional business had achieved only 70 percent of the time, stabilized above 99 percent. Still better, SQA's sales growth rose to 25 percent per year, three times the industry average.

We tell the Herman Miller story to make an important point—that strategy in the absence of effective implementation is pointless. Some believe that strategy is actually less important than implementation in the sense that strategy is becoming a commodity in many industries—something that any rival can duplicate. In this case strategy is not a tool for differentiation. What matters more than strategy, in their opinion, is the ability to execute exceptionally well. Stanford's Jeffrey Pfeffer puts it this way: "It is more important to manage your business right than to be in the right business."[2] Success, in his view, comes from successfully implementing one's strategy, not just having one. The ideal, of course, is to have both a great strategy and outstanding implementation!

Getting from strategy to implementation requires attention to a number of structural, personnel, and resource issues. (See "The Seven S Framework" for one possible model for strategy implementation.) Any successful strategy must be formed around a coherent and reinforcing set of supporting practices and structures. Most people call this *alignment*. For a business, alignment is a situation in which organizational structures, support systems, processes, human skills, resources, and incentives support strategic goals. In their excellent book on this subject, George Labovitz and Victor Rosansky identify four elements of alignment: strategy, processes, people (employees), and customers. "When the four elements of alignment are simultaneously connected," they write, "each element is supported and strengthened by the others . . . and great things happen."[3]

Declaring a strategy won't get you far if you fail to create alignment between it and the many large and small things that constitute how your company operates. Companies that fail to achieve alignment fail to get the results they seek. This chapter examines elements of alignment that implementers must consider.

The Seven S Framework

Over the years, attempts have been made to create a model for successful strategy implementation. One of the first—and best—of these first appeared in *The Art of Japanese Management*, authored by Richard Pascale and Anthony Athos and published in 1981. Their model was adopted by McKinsey & Company, a global strategy consulting organization; many now refer to it as the McKinsey Seven S Framework. The "S" in this framework are Strategy, Structure, Systems, Style, Staff, Skills, and Superordinate goals. If you'd like to learn more about this framework for strategy implementation, refer to Richard Pascale's *Managing on the Edge*. (See "For Further Reading" at the end of this book for the bibliographic details.)

Elements of strategy alignment involve people, incentives, supportive activities, organizational structure, culture, and the leadership of the business, as represented in figure 5-1. Notice in that figure how each element is aligned with strategic goals and with each of the other elements, forming a solid platform for implementation and eventual success.

FIGURE 5-1

Alignment for Implementation

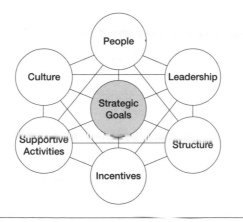

People and Incentives

Every manager and every employee—from the executive suite to the loading dock—must be involved with implementation. Senior management has a responsibility to communicate strategic intent to employees, and mid- and lower-level managers must reiterate that intent and translate it into the way their subordinates work. Management must also ensure that the company has:

- People with the right skills to make the strategy successful (this is accomplished through hiring and training)

- People with attitudes that support the strategy

- The resources that people need to do their jobs well

Companies don't always get the people side of implementation right. Consultant/author Dwight Gertz has described one company that operated a chain of fresh-baked cookie shops in shopping malls and other high-traffic areas across the United States. Years of experience had helped management learn which cookies to bake, when, in what quantities. Its executives knew that if store managers simply followed their published operating procedures, sales and profits would follow—they always had.

Unfortunately, the cookie company's human resource department was advertising for store manager candidates with the theme of "Be your own boss." Not surprisingly, this attracted entrepreneurial people who wanted to run things their own way. That would be just fine in some situations, but not this one. These people didn't follow the company's success formula, and, not surprisingly, profitability plummeted where the new entrepreneurial recruits ran things. They made the wrong cookies, or they made too few or too many at different times of the day or week.[4]

In this case, the company had a sound strategy and a proven set of operating procedures. But its personnel selection process was out of alignment; it was hiring people who were temperamentally indisposed to follow those procedures. The mind-set of key employees was not aligned with the company's formula for making money; instead, it was neutralizing the power of the company's formula.

Incentives are another big part of the people side of implementation—and perhaps the most important factor in implementation overall. Unless employees have real incentives to implement the strategy, they will not commit to it, and the strategy will probably fail. Have you ever worked in a situation in which there were few incentives to work toward key goals? A financial services company, for example, wanted to differentiate itself from local competitors by promising top-quality financial planning services delivered by knowledgeable customer-facing personnel. In a field in which all competitors offered basically the same products and services, this strategy aimed to attract the most valuable customers (i.e., high-net-worth individuals and families). To implement the strategy, this company needed employees who had substantial training and experience in financial planning. Unfortunately, this company's incentive system failed to support the strategy. People with advanced training were not paid any more than their peers; nor was greater experience rewarded. Consequently, highly trained and experienced customer-facing employees routinely left to join other firms—where their skills earned higher pay. They were replaced with inexperienced personnel, a practice that undermined the company's strategy. (See "The Say-Do Problem" for a further examination of strategy/implementation misalignment.)

The best assurance of implementation is a rewards system that aligns employees' interests with the success of the strategy. That is nothing more than common sense. To accomplish this, every unit and every employee should have measurable performance goals with clearly stated rewards for goal achievement. And the rewards should be large enough to elicit the desired level of employee effort.

Where does your company stand on the people part of strategy? Do its incentive programs and HR practices measurably support the strategy? Do its hiring and training practices aim to get the right people with the right skills into positions where they can make a difference? Does it have a say-do problem?

The Say-Do Problem

Misalignment between incentives and strategy is often the result of what experts at Mercer Human Resources Consulting describe as the "say-do" problem. A company says one thing but does another. As described in a study of human capital measurement, these experts cite the example of one high-tech company that touted its pay-for-performance policy. Examination of company HR data, however, indicated something entirely different: Only 5 percent of total pay was directly linked to individual performance. In fact, people in the lowest quartile of performance were getting almost as much from the annual bonus pool as the company's top performers.

Similar say-do contradictions were found in other companies. In each instance, incentive mechanisms were failing to support explicit company strategies and goals. Does your company suffer from the say-do problem?

SOURCE: Haig Nalbantian, Richard Guzzo, Dave Kieffer, and Jay Doherty, *Play to Your Strengths* (New York: McGraw-Hill, 2004), 36–43.

Supportive Activities

Misalignment on the human resources front is a common impediment to effective implementation. But there are others, including activities that few of us would think essential to the success of a particular strategy. Corporate-level strategy, according to Harvard professors David Collis and Cynthia Montgomery, "is a system of interdependent parts. Its success depends not only on the quality of the individual elements but also on how the elements reinforce each other."[5] Michael Porter has used the example of Southwest Airlines to illustrate how success is more likely when many seemingly unrelated activities reinforce each other and the overall strategy: "Southwest's . . . competitive advantage comes from the way its activities fit and reinforce one another."[6] For example, the company's strategy is to compete on the basis of low-cost, frequent service. As figure 5-2 illustrates, many primary activities make that strategy feasible, and

FIGURE 5-2

Southwest Airlines' Activity System

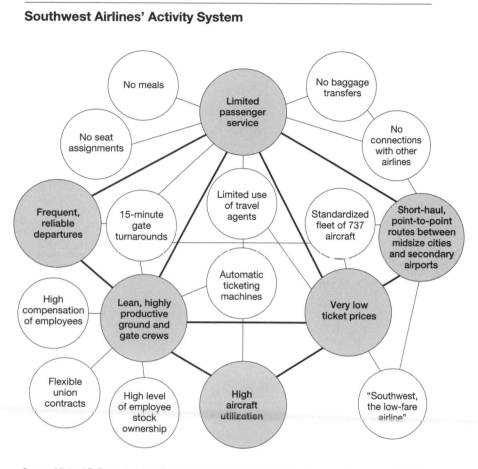

Source: Michael E. Porter, "What Is Strategy," *Harvard Business Review,* November–December 1996, 73. Reproduced with permission.

these are supported by other activities. Keeping ticket prices very low, for instance, is a primary activity of the strategy; it is supported by high aircraft utilization, the limited use of travel agents, a standardized fleet of aircraft, highly productive ground crews, and so forth. In the absence of any one of these linking activities, Southwest's low-cost strategy would be jeopardized. But together they make it work. Southwest's traditional rivals have periodically tried to emulate its strategy by offering low fares and frequent departures, but because they lack supportive activities, all have failed. According to Porter, "Southwest's activities complement one another in ways that create real economic value. . . .That is the way strategic fit creates competitive advantage and superior profitability."[7]

Take a minute to review your own strategy and ask, How well is it supported by the organization's other key activities? For example, if rapid and accurate order fulfillment is a key element of your strategy—as in the Herman Miller case described above—you'd want to coordinate sales, order-processing, manufacturing, and delivery activities, and purge them of errors and wasted time. Do hiring, training, logistics, pricing, and other activities create an interlocking support system for strategy? If they don't, what could be done to link strategy and these supportive activities more effectively?

Organizational Structure

Successful military leaders have always organized their forces in terms of their battlefield strategies. In the first days of World War II, for example, German army commanders opted for a strategy of blitzkrieg—highly mobile, or "lightning," warfare. This strategy aimed to counter the static trench warfare strategy that their Belgian and French rivals had carried over from World War I. Speed, surprise, air support, and the concentrated power of fast-moving armored units were the key elements of the new German strategy. Instead of slogging it out from fixed positions in a long battle of attrition—as both sides had done in World War I—the Germans aimed to pierce or outflank fixed defenses, causing havoc and collapse in the enemy's rear. In some cases, paratroopers would be dropped behind or on enemy flanks to produce a similar result.

This new battlefield strategy demanded a new organization. Instead of the traditional model of deploying a small armored unit in support of the much larger infantry, the roles were reversed. Armor formed the tip of the spear; infantry, artillery, and supply units were organized in its support. Each of those support units was mechanized to keep pace with the fast-moving armor, and all were linked through field communications.

The blitzkrieg strategy was the main contributor to Germany's victories early in World War II. U.S. General George Patton was among the first on the Allied side to appreciate its power, and he is credited with reorganizing his own forces to meet and defeat mobile German armies in North Africa, Sicily, and France.

As much as business people like to see military analogies in what they are doing, business is not warfare. Nevertheless, the military example of reorganizing people and material in support of a new strategy is instructive and useful. Our earlier story about Herman Miller makes it clear that that company would not have succeeded in its strategy of fast, dependable delivery of mass-customized office workstations and furniture without a reorganization of its human, supplier, and manufacturing assets. Like every other enterprise that pursues agility and speed, Miller had to shift the work into a lean, nonhierarchical unit in which production decisions could be made swiftly and monitored more effectively.

Take a minute or so now to think about your company's organization. Are its people, resources, and units aligned with company strategy? How about in your own unit? Company strategy has created goals for your unit—these are your contributions to the top-level strategy. Is your unit optimally organized to achieve those goals? If it isn't, what could you do to make it so?

Culture and Leadership

Culture and leadership are the last elements of strategy implementation you need to consider. These must be supportive of both the strategy and the day-to-day work that implements it.

Business literature refers often to company culture. We have, for instance, many references to 3M's culture of innovation and its 15 Percent Rule, which allows R&D personnel to spend 15 percent of their time pursuing whatever ideas appeal to them, as long as they have some commercial potential. We also hear of Wal-Mart's culture of dedication to customer satisfaction and driving down costs. And then there's eBay's more playful, collegial, and "can-do" culture.

Culture refers to a company's values, traditions, and operating style. It is one of those vague qualities that is difficult to measure or describe with precision, but it nevertheless exists and sets the tone for managerial and employee behavior. In a sense the term describes how people view their workplace and how things are done. One company may be highly male and engineering-oriented, pride itself on its tradition of technical innovation and problem solving, and operate with a command-and-control style. Another company's culture, in contrast, may be gender-neutral, value service quality above all else, and operate in a collegial, nonhierarchical manner.

One way to understand a company's culture is to ask, "Who are your company's heroes, and what stories do people tell about them?" These heroes might be super-salespeople, or master organizers, such as General Motors' Alfred Sloan. St. Paul–based 3M Company counts Dick Drew and William McKnight among its heroes, and even though these individuals passed from the scene many decades ago, current employees know who they were, recognize their contributions, and tell their stories.

Dick Drew, the developer of masking and cellophane adhesive tapes in the 1920s and 1930s, was an accomplished inventor—a man who could both recognize a customer problem and craft a profitable technical solution. His many successful products made him a legend within the company. William McKnight spent his entire career (1907–1966) with the company, eventually rising from assistant bookkeeper to president, and then chairman. McKnight's great contribution to 3M lore was as a business philosopher whose management principles continue to guide the company. He described that philosophy as follows:

> *As our business grows, it becomes increasingly necessary to delegate responsibility and to encourage men and women to exercise their initiative. This requires considerable tolerance. Those men and women, to whom we delegate authority and responsibility, if they are good people, are going to want to do their jobs in their own way.*
>
> *Mistakes will be made. But if a person is essentially right, the mistakes he or she makes are not as serious in the long run as the mistakes*

management will make if it undertakes to tell those in authority exactly how they must do their jobs.

Management that is destructively critical when mistakes are made kills initiative. And it's essential that we have many people with initiative if we are to continue to grow.[8]

Culture may be strong or weak. Strong cultures are difficult to change without great effort, time, and substantial disruption. Thus, companies with strong cultures are wise to adopt strategies consistent with their cultures. Doing otherwise creates implementation problems. For example, it is advisable for 3M, Hewlett-Packard, Nokia, and Siemens to stick to strategies consistent with their cultures of technical innovation; their cultures will naturally support implementation. Companies that find themselves in competitively dead-end positions, however, may have to adopt strategies that are at odds with their existing cultures. The traditional air carriers (United, BOAC, Delta, and so forth) are prime examples of companies that must change their strategies or go under. Yet the strategic options before them will require a difficult set of cultural changes. For some, the "us versus them" culture of contentious labor relations problems will have to give way to something more collaborative. In these cases, culture and strategy must be reinvented simultaneously—a truly difficult proposition.

Changing company culture to better align it with a new strategy is the responsibility of the CEO and the senior management team. It is a top-down job. Here are a few ideas for approaching the task:

- Identify the aspects of culture that must change in support of strategy implementation—for example, product quality, greater customer focus, the elimination of command-and-control management. Concentrate on these and leave less critical aspects of culture alone. You can only do so much.

- Model the behaviors and values that you'd like employees to adopt. For example, if you aim for greater customer focus, visibly spend more of your time visiting customers. Bring the most imaginative and demanding users of your products into the company for focus group discussion with employees. If adopting a low-cost model is called for, cut your own travel and entertainment expenses before you ask others to do the same. Remember, people are watching you.

- Engage employees in "town meeting" forums to build consensus and commitment to change. A personal connection between the leadership and rank-and-file employees is essential.

- Sponsor celebratory events when change milestones are met.

- Set high performance standards.

- Reward people for the results you seek.

How well aligned is your company with its chosen strategy? Do you have the right people and clear incentives? Is your organization structured in a way that supports the strategy? Do other key activities support the strategy? Do your business culture and business strategy fit well together? Table 5-1 is a checklist you can use to re-

TABLE 5-1

Alignment Checklist

		Yes	No
People	Our people have the necessary skills to make the strategy work		
	They support the strategy		
	Their attitudes are aligned with the strategy		
	They have the resources they need to be successful		
Incentives	Our rewards system is aligned with the strategy		
	Everyone has performance goals aligned with the strategy		
Structure	Units are optimally organized to support the strategy		
Supportive activities	The many things we do around here—pricing, the way we handle customers, fulfill orders, etc.—support the strategy		
Culture	Our culture and strategy are well matched		

For every "no" response, specify the problem and what needs to be done to correct it:

view the alignment concepts explained in this chapter and to answer these questions.

Summing Up

- Implementation describes the concrete measures that translate strategic intent into actions that produce results. It requires continuous managerial attention at all levels.

- Successful strategy is aligned with a coherent and reinforcing set of supporting practices and structures.

- Alignment is a situation in which organizational structures, support systems, processes, human skills, resources, and incentives support strategic goals.

- Be sure that you have the people with the skills, resources, and attitudes to make the strategy work.

- Activities such as pricing, distribution, order fulfillment, and the like should support the strategy.

- Structure the organization to align with strategic goals.

- The organization's culture should be appropriate for the strategy—and vice versa.

6

Action Plans

The Architecture of Implementation

Key Topics Covered in This Chapter

- *Agreeing on goals*

- *Adopting performance measures*

- *Determining the who, what, and when of getting the work done*

- *Determining the level and type of resources needed to do the job*

- *Identifying all important interlocks between units and outside entities*

- *Making a financial estimate of the plan's impact*

SUCCESSFUL IMPLEMENTATION IS accomplished by turning strategic plans into action plans that are executed at the unit level. Those action plans must address key strategic goals through practical steps, measure progress over time, assure that people have the resources they need, and keep everything on track.

An action plan is where strategic planning and implementation overlap. It is also where mid-level managers can really make important and visible contributions to organizational success. This chapter segments the action-planning process into a number of key steps. Once each of those steps is explained, we'll present an example of one company's formal action plan. You can use that as a prototype for your own action planning.[1]

From Strategic Plan to Unit Action Plans

An *action plan* is a document that begins with strategic goals and identifies all the steps required to achieve them. This is represented graphically in figure 6-1. Here, each of a company's three operating units has determined its unique contributions to the company's strategic goals. These contributions, in turn, become unit goals, which each unit aims to achieve through a set of measurable action steps. Consider this example:

Pedalpower Bicycle Company (PBC) had developed a new strategy for expanding its sales in the fragmented North American bicycle market. It will target the profitable upper tier of street bikes. PBC bikes will be designed to appeal to quality-conscious adult cyclists who regularly pedal to work or use their bikes for errands around town or simply for recreation. Consequently, PBC bikes will be rugged and come equipped with wide, puncture-proof tires, chain guards (to protect trousers from oily chains), and detachable fenders for rainy day riding. Racers, trail-bikers, and kids are not in the target market. The strategy calls for unit sales of 400,000 by the end of the third year.

To further differentiate themselves, the new PBC products will feature a modular design, making it possible for consumers and dealers to customize their orders and have them delivered quickly. This customization strategy has been successfully implemented in Japan and South

FIGURE 6-1

Unit Goals, Metrics, and Action Plans

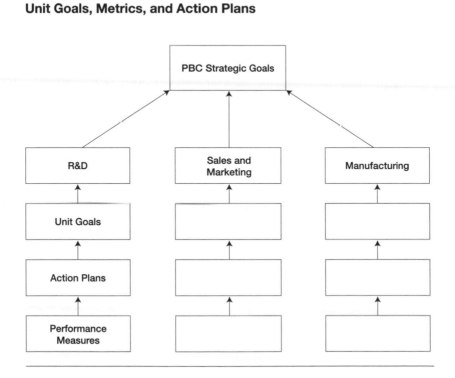

*Korea by an Asian manufacturer, but has not been applied to PBC's
target market in North America.*

*Though every unit of PBC will have to contribute to the strategy
through specific implementation plans, three units in particular will be
most affected: product development; sales and marketing; and manufacturing. Product development sets four goals for itself:*

1. *Work with marketing to determine customer requirements and pricing constraints by January 2, 2006.*

2. *Based on Goal 1 results, design three prototypes for market testing
   by April 1, 2006.*

3. *Based on Goal 2 results, create manufacturing specifications for three
   customizable models by August 1, 2006.*

4. *Concurrently work with manufacturing on design for manufacturability. Deliverable: A list of no more than sixty components capable of
   producing several thousand uniquely configured bikes. Deadline: October 1, 2006.*

Notice in this example how PBC's product development unit
has translated the company's strategy goal into specific, measurable
unit goals. The product development manager and her team will
then develop specific action plans around each goal. The sales and
marketing, manufacturing, and other operating units will do something very similar, and their collective goals of product development,
sales and marketing, and manufacturing will then be rolled up into a
complete implementation plan.

Set Goals

A company's mission and strategic goals are the natural starting point
for corporate- and unit-level goals. These should determine how the
organization as a whole will direct its efforts over a multiyear period.
Individual units take companywide strategic goals and deconstruct
them into unit goals with clear targets and performance measures.
For example, a direct-mail sporting goods company might have a

strategic goal of gaining a 15 percent market share within three years. For its part, the company's customer service unit would then create its own goal: to raise its customer satisfaction index from 73 to 90 percent over the next two years, and to 95 percent by the end of the third year. Meanwhile the marketing department might come up with a unit goal of increasing customer loyalty by 20 percent during the same three-year period, while the national sales force would focus on increasing average account revenue by 15 percent as a unit goal. The action plans of these different units might have a common goal of developing a new customer database by the end of Year 1.

In effect, the company's highest strategic goals cascade down to the units, which devise goals for their parts of the strategy, as described in figure 6-1. Unit managers respond through the performance goals they negotiate with each of their teams or direct reports, as described in figure 6-2.

Top management must examine unit goals to assure itself that they:

- Support and are compatible with the company's strategy

- Add up to a complete plan for achieve the company's strategic goals

Management must be alert for unit goals that are in conflict with those of the company or those of other units. It must also ensure that

FIGURE 6-2

Linking Corporate, Unit, and Team/Individual Goals

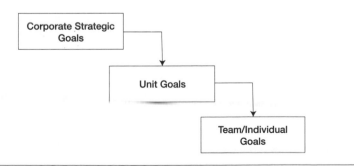

all the initiatives required to achieve company goals are covered within the collective unit plans.

Agree on Performance Measures

Once you settle on goals and a plan to reach them, your unit must find ways to measure its performance in terms of those goals. The metrics of performance should be relevant and clear—for example, "Increase market penetration by 10 percent annually for the next five years in Latin American countries." Performance metrics should also address factors that you can actually measure without breaking the bank. For instance, in the above example, you might ask: "Would we be able to accurately measure market penetration throughout Latin America without breaking our budget? It's a big continent with many local and regional markets."

There are many systems for measuring performance. Managers have traditionally looked to accounting measures as performance indicators. Key among these are revenues from sales, sales-per-employee, gross profits, profit margin, return on invested capital, and return on assets. These are more useful at the enterprise level than as measures of unit performance relative to action plans. Here are examples of performance areas that might be measured by three different corporate units:

MARKETING UNIT	MANUFACTURING UNIT	HUMAN RESOURCES UNIT
Sales	Unit volume	Training
Market share	Cost	Recruiting
New-product sales	Efficiency	Employee turnover
Pricing	Quality	Regulatory
Distribution	Process improvement	compliance
	Process innovation	Compensation/wages

Once the result for a unit's critical areas of performance has been determined, the next step is to decide how success will be measured.

Based on those measures, unit objectives can be defined. For example, for a manufacturing unit, two key performance areas and their corresponding measures and objectives might be:

KEY PERFORMANCE AREA	MEASURES	OBJECTIVES
Cost	Cost per unit	• By end of Year 1, cost per unit will be $79.50 • By end of Year 2, cost per unit will be $71.00
	Units per employee per year	• By end of Year 1, units per employee per year will be 15,000 • By end of Year 2, units per employee per year will be 24,000
Safety	Work time loss per year (hours)	• By end of Year 1, work time loss per year will be 25 hours • By end of Year 2, work time loss per year will be 10 hours
	Plant safety index	• By end of Year 1, plant safety index will be 94 • By end of Year 2, plant safety index will be 98

Whichever performance measurement system your company or unit uses, you need measures that are specific, measurable, achievable, realistic, and time-bound. Here are some examples of unit measures that meet those criteria, along with others that do not:

GOOD MEASURES	NOT-SO-GOOD MEASURES
Add 20 new systems engineers in the next three years who are capable of handling the new programming language. Year 1, add 2 new people; Year 2, add 9 new people; Year 3, add 9 new people.	Add new systems engineers who are capable of handling the new advanced programming language. (Not specific, measurable, or time-bound.)

Good Measures	Not-So-Good Measures
Raise sales 10 percent annually over the next three years.	Improve sales over the next year. (Not specific or measurable.)
Reduce average duration of customer service phone calls by 40 percent over the next two years.	Reduce average duration of customer service phone calls by 90 percent over the next year (Probably not achievable or realistic.)

Formulate Action Steps

Once specific, measurable, achievable, realistic, and time-bound goals have been assigned at the unit level, the question is: How will we achieve these goals? The answer is through *action steps*. Action steps are the "who," "what," and "when" of carrying out a strategic initiative and achieving assigned goals. The sum of these steps should complete the job.

In approaching a goal, ask this question: What are all the steps that must be taken to accomplish our goal? Once you have the answer, ask this question for each step you've identified: Can this step be broken down into sub-steps? By asking that same question over and over for each step and its component sub-steps, you will eventually reach a point where steps can no longer be subdivided. At that point, you will have identified every action step. Project managers use this approach all the time to assure that they've scoped the job and all its associated tasks. They use the term *work breakdown structure*. They go further by estimating the amount of time required for each step. Here's an example from the bicycle company case; it covers just one major step, which is then broken down into sub-steps, with their estimated execution times. (Note: For a blank work structure breakdown worksheet, see the appendix. A downloadable version is available on the Harvard Business Essentials Web site: www.elearning .hbsp.org/businesstools.)

Major Step (or task)	Level 1 Sub-steps	Level 2 Sub-steps	Level 2 Sub-step Duration (hours)
Test prototype bike	Select subjects	Identify 12 possible subjects	5
		Solicit and confirm participation	4
	Set up a test routine	Determine which features to test and how	2
		Develop an objective testing routine	3

Every step should have an "owner" who publicly agrees to take responsibility for it. Steps that lack clear owners are often done haphazardly or left undone.

Determine the Resources Needed

An action plan is not complete if it fails to recognize the resources a unit needs to implement its share of the strategy. Action plan resources typically include many of the following:

- People
- Technologies
- Support from other departments
- Time

- Money (per budget)
- Office space
- Strategic partners
- Training

Managers often make the mistake of underestimating their resource needs. Those who fail to determine realistic needs or take shortcuts run the risk of having too few of the resources needed to execute their plans successfully. Here are some questions a manager might ask when assessing resource needs:

- How will this new action plan impact my group's ongoing day-to-day work?

- Can the existing resources cover the action plan in addition to business-as-usual?

- If not, what additional resources will the unit need?

- What new skills will our people need to execute the plan?

- What training will be required, and at what cost?

- What new systems or technology will we need to support the initiative? At what cost?

As you think about the resources your unit needs, remember to look beyond what the group needs today and consider what it might require in the coming years. By forecasting skills and competencies needed in the future and by hiring for "tomorrow," a unit can keep pace with the market and build a competitive advantage. For example, suppose your company's long-term strategy calls for leveraging an up-and-coming technology—and designing new products using that technology. You may anticipate a need for team members skilled in the technology a year down the road. In this case, you might train some employees in that technology *now* to lay the foundation for handling work that will come later.

Planning ahead, thinking strategically, and leveraging current resources are key management skills in a world of constrained resources. Your aim should be to end up with everyone and everything you need by the time you need them.

Identify Interlocks

Few units work effectively in isolation. They need to collaborate with others—both inside and outside the company—to accomplish their goals. We refer to these points of cross-functional collaboration as *in-*

terlocks. Interlocks don't appear on organizational charts, but they nevertheless play an important role in getting work done. Interlocks can take the form of a task force, an interdepartmental team, or individuals within a department who work together. A growing percentage of work in business organizations is now completed through interlocks.

Interlocks result in two different types of exchanges: giving and receiving. Sometimes, units will need to receive work from other units in order to complete their action plans. At other times, units will need to give work to other units so that the latter can implement their own action plans. Typically, several groups need to collaborate to carry out a strategic initiative, and the interlocks can be substantial. Let's suppose, for example, that our company needs to focus on market share with the goal of growing its market share by 30 percent over the next five years. This corporate goal will likely have an impact on many (if not all) units in the company. In developing action plans, units throughout the organization will find that they need to collaborate to implement their plans. Here are some potential interlocks:

IF YOUR UNIT IS ...	YOU MIGHT NEED ...	FOR HELP IN ...
Sales	Human resources personnel	Designing a series of courses on effective cross-selling
Marketing	Information technology	Building a customer database that distinguishes market segments
Product Development	Finance	Clarifying new business models

As collaboration across units and departments increases, companies often form cross-functional teams comprising representatives from each of the units that have interlocking interests and obligations. Using the above example, a company may decide that the goal necessitates creating a cross-functional team. In this case, the team might be led by someone from marketing and include others from product development, sales, and information technology. The team might enlist representatives from finance and human resources as needed, perhaps as ex-office team members.

When cross-functional teams are created, they typically develop a charter that outlines the group's roles, responsibilities, key milestones, deliverables, and decision-making processes.

Interlocks complicate managerial control, the assignment of resources, and accountability. Managers often find interlocks challenging for the simple reason that they lack formal authority over the people involved. A cross-functional team, for example, may be led by the representative of one function who has no power to discipline or reward its members—some of whom may enjoy higher rank in the organization. He or she must lead without benefit of formal power or authority. As for resources, people must look to each member of an interlock and assure that their combined resources are up to the job. This should be done in the early planning stage.

To ensure accountability, it is wise for managers to document all interlock needs, expectations, and obligations. If an interlock agreement cannot be reached, it should be identified as an area of risk in the action plan.

Failure to agree on interlock arrangements can be a source of a conflict between groups in organizations—especially when resources are tight. For example, a marketing manager may approach the head of information systems and explain that he needs help:

> *"We need a database to keep track of all customers and to record all transactions in what we call the 'active seniors' segment. Our goal is to expand that segment by 25 percent over the next two years. Could one of your people become a regular member of the task force we've set up to address that goal? We plan to meet once every two weeks over the coming year."*

But the head of IS might answer:

> *"I'd like to help but, frankly, I can't spare anyone. We have our own goals, you know."*

Conflicts that arise during implementation need to be surfaced immediately in order to keep action plans on course. ("Tips for Crafting Your Action Plan" offers further advice for developing a plan that can avoid some of these problems.)

Tips for Crafting Your Action Plan

- **Keep it simple.** An overly complex plan will confuse and frustrate. So if your flow chart of activities looks like the wiring diagram for the space shuttle, revise it with an eye toward simplicity and coherence.

- **Involve the people who will execute the plan.** Implementation plans are more likely to succeed if they are not simply imposed on the people asked to push them forward. If the implementers are involved in developing the action plan, they'll be more dedicated to its success. Remember, too, that a plan devised solely by senior-level strategists is less likely to reflect the realities of the business and what the organization can accomplish than a plan built on the ideas of the people on the front line—the people who do the work.

- **Structure your action plan in achievable chunks.** Overly ambitious plans are usually doomed to failure. People look at them and say, "We'll never get this done—not in our lifetimes." They'll be defeated from the beginning. So build an action plan that is both manageable and achievable.

- **Specify roles and responsibilities.** Like every endeavor, an action plan should detail clear roles and responsibilities. Every planned outcome should be the acknowledged responsibility of one or more individuals. Those individuals should publicly state that they accept their roles. Doing so puts them on record as taking responsibility for results.

- **Make it flexible.** Business strategies seldom follow planned trajectories or timetables. Competitors counterattack. Customers don't behave as anticipated. Bad things happen. Thus, a good implementation plan is a living document open to revision. Organizations that lock themselves into rigid schedules, goals, and events ultimately find themselves detached from the shifting world in which they must do business.

Estimate the Financial Impact

The final piece of the unit action plan is an estimate of the costs associated with the plan. For example, if a customer service department has the goal of increasing its customer satisfaction index by 10 percent, and if it knows that two additional personnel and training for every person who contacts customers will be needed, the department should develop a clear estimate of the added cost. Some units, such as the sales department, would also estimate the incremental revenue anticipated from plan implementation and the incremental cost of obtaining it.

A Sample Action Plan

Now that we've discussed all key parts of the unit action plan, let's wrap them up into a sample, in this case for the manufacturing unit of an electronics company.

GOALS. Develop long-range manufacturing facilities that will:

- meet forecast demand from 2007–2013;
- accommodate testing and the manufacture of new products; and
- achieve dramatic improvement in quality, cost, and customer service.

PERFORMANCE METRICS. Agree on performance measures that are both relevant and clear.

- Year 1: Complete the design phase and begin construction by year-end.
- Year 2: Complete construction and start-up production by year-end.
- Year 3: Achieve initial running rate of 177 million units per year at a cost of $0.325 per unit.

ACTION STEPS. Break your plan down into achievable action steps. (The following steps have been simplified for purposes of illustration.)

YEAR 1

What	Who	When
Establish plant design specifications	Manufacturing team; engineering leads	October 2005
Approve specifications	Senior management	December 2005
Flow chart and production system design; costing	Manufacturing team; engineering and finance lead	April 2006
Detailed drawings for bid purposes; costing	Manufacturing team; engineering and finance lead	July 2006
Approval	Senior management	August 2006
Bids	Purchasing and construction	October 2006
Construction starts	Construction team from manufacturing and facilities takes over	December 2006

RESOURCES. Hire one full-time construction manager, two plant managers from groundbreaking on, and three assistants to support these managers.

INTERLOCKS. Identify the ways units will have to work with each other. (The following has been simplified for purposes of illustration.)

MANUFACTURING UNIT WORKS WITH . . .	TO . . .	WHEN
Construction unit	Manage entire construction process	Start January 2007
Legal	Handle all licenses, liability assessment, and insurance	Start December 2006
Customers	Form customer service committee to design order-entry shipment systems	Start May 2006

FINANCIAL IMPACT ESTIMATE. Develop a long-term estimate detailing costs and revenues.

Cost: Expense capital = $125 million
                     Capital = $125 million
                     Equipment = $250 million
                     Total investment = $500 million

		Year 1	Year 3	Year 5
Revenue	Price/unit	$0.425	$0.400	$0.350
(new plant):	Cost/unit	$0.325	$0.270	$0.180
	Units	$177M	$525M	$700M
	Revenue	$75M	$210M	$500M

As you can see, an action plan is a rational, building-block approach to getting a big job done. It begins with the top-tier question, what are we trying to accomplish? It then systematically gathers the resources and creates all the mechanisms required to do the job.

Unfortunately, even the best-conceived action plan is vulnerable to unforeseen events, conflicts, and people problems that can make it run off the tracks. The manager's job is to assure that action plans stay on track and stay aligned with strategy. That is the subject of our next chapter.

Summing Up

- An implementation action plan begins with strategic goals and identifies all the steps required to achieve them.

- Action planning begins at the top, with company goals, and cascades down through the organization by defining the measurable action steps that units and subunits will contribute to those top-level goals.

- Make the company's mission and strategic goals the natural starting point for corporate and unit-level goals.

- Once you settle on goals and a plan to reach them, your unit must find ways to measure its performance in terms of those goals. Performance metrics should be specific, measurable, achievable, realistic, and time-bound.

- The best approach to goal achievement is through action steps—the "who," "what," and "when" of carrying out a strategic initiative and achieving assigned goals. The sum of these steps should complete the job.

- Make sure that every action step has an "owner" who publicly agrees to take responsibility for it. Steps that lack clear owners are often done haphazardly or left undone.

- If you are an action step "owner," be sure that you have all the resources (time, money, people, training, etc.) needed to get the job done.

- Most organization work involves interlocks, or points of cross-functional collaboration.

- Make an estimate of the costs associated with your action plan.

7

How to Stay on Course

Sensing and Responding to Deviations from Plan

Key Topics Covered in This Chapter

- *A practical model for successful implementation*

- *Using progress reviews to monitor implementation*

- *The value of informal checks by executives and managers*

- *Some common causes of implementation failure*

- *How contingency plans can address potential setbacks*

SET IT AND forget it? That might be possible with a fine timepiece, but not with strategy implementation. Action plans provide instructions for achieving specific goals, but people don't always follow instructions. Or they misinterpret those instructions. Or their instructions fail to address all workplace and market realities. Or something in the environment—over which you have no control—changes. No action plan can foresee the many obstacles and changing conditions that people will face over the weeks and months it takes to implement a strategy. Thus, midcourse adjustments and management intervention are inevitable and necessary. This chapter offers suggestions for keeping implementation on course.[1]

A Model for Staying on Course

Not every strategic plan succeeds. Several months after a new strategic initiative is launched, both management and employees may sense that things aren't working out as anticipated. Goals are being missed. Financial results aren't even close to what planners had anticipated. The first instinct is to blame the new strategy and the people who cooked it up: "Whatever made them think that this strategy would put us in a stronger position?" Indeed, the plan may be ill-conceived, but it's equally likely that implementation has gone off track. As Larry Bossidy and Ram Charan write in their popular book, *Execution*: "[T]he strategy by itself is not often the cause. Strategies most often fail because they aren't executed well."[2]

If you've been around for a while you can probably remember strategic initiatives that never delivered what they promised. What caused these plans to fall short of expectations? Was the problem in the strategy or in how your company implemented it?

Assuming that a company has done a good job of developing action plans around each strategic goal, it can avoid failure by closely tracking plan implementation and addressing unanticipated problems. If it identifies small problems and pounces on them before they can grow into big problems, there's a good chance that it can get back on track. Figure 7-1 shows a straightforward model for accomplishing this. In the model, management at different levels is continuously

FIGURE 7-1

Finding and Fixing Implementation Problems

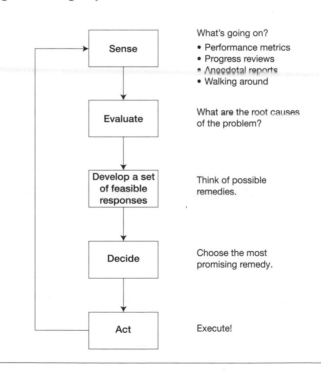

sensing for deviations from action plans, or for plans that are falling short of expectations. Its sensing tools are:

- The performance metrics built into each action plan

- Periodic progress reviews

- Anecdotal reports from people on the scene

- Direct observation by managers who learn by "walking around"

Sensing produces data that management and implementation teams can use to evaluate the situation. What is going wrong? What are the root causes of implementation problems? Evaluation naturally leads to potential remedies. Brainstorming among implementers can often produce one or more ways to fix problems and remove barriers to success. The next steps are to select and execute the remedy most likely to get implementation back on track.

Progress Review

Periodic progress review is a powerful tool for monitoring implementation. Review, using the performance metrics built into each action step, makes it possible for managers to gauge how well people are doing relative to plan. Consider this example, based on the bicycle maker we met in the previous chapter:

> *Pedalpower Bicycle Company (PBC) launched its new strategy of developing and selling customizable, adult street bikes three months ago. As its part of the strategy, the product development unit had developed an action plan with four goals:*
>
> *1. Work with marketing to determine customer requirements and pricing constraints by January 2, 2006.*
>
> *2. Based on Goal 1 results, design three prototypes for market testing by April 1, 2006.*

3. *Based on Goal 2 results, create manufacturing specifications for three customizable models by August 1, 2006.*

4. *Concurrently work with manufacturing on design for manufacturability. Deliverable: A list of no more than sixty components capable of producing several thousand uniquely configured bikes. Deadline: October 1, 2006.*

Unfortunately, by late February 2006, the product development unit wasn't even close to accomplishing its second goal: creating three prototypes. Falling short of that goal would put other unit goals behind schedule, and would upset the entire timetable for breaking into the market. The product development manager has explained it this way: "We cannot move ahead with designs until we have a solid set of customer requirements. We've been working with the marketing people to get these, but it's taking longer than we anticipated."

So, if market research is the problem, why is that? "We've been too short-handed to do focus group sessions or to talk to all the dealers we planned to visit," says the head of marketing. "We had enough resources when we wrote our action plan, but then Brenda left the company, and we've haven't been able to find a suitable person to replace her."

The problems encountered by product development and marketing in this example are all plausible. The question is, why has so much time slipped by without these problems being identified and corrected? Weekly or monthly progress reviews are the best mechanisms for catching problems like the one that now jeopardizes PBC's strategy implementation. Had PBC instituted this type of review, marketing's personnel shortages would have been spotted early, before the larger, schedule-busting problem developed. This would have given management an opportunity to deal with the root problems.

What sort of oversight does your company provide for important activities? If its oversight is weak, which are the optimal points at which it should be strengthened?

Use Performance Measures to Pace Progress

As described in the previous chapter, every important implementation goal—at the company and unit level—should be linked to one or more performance measures: manufacturing costs per unit, sales per sales representative, cycle time for completing a business process, and so forth. And, as stated earlier, each of these should have a time component: for example, "Customer requirements should be determined by _____ ." Unit managers should use these metrics and dates to identify where progress is and is not being made. Metrics indicating that implementation isn't moving in the right direction—or moving too slowly—should signal managers to intervene, find the sources of the problem, and fix them. And remember, it's always easier to fix problems that are caught earlier than later.

Quarterly Reviews

Formal quarterly reviews are another important tool for assessing progress and assuring that action plans are being implemented. Typically, units or teams submit one- to two-page reports to senior management for each of the action plans they are implementing. These reports address the following points:

1. What the unit has accomplished

2. What the unit hasn't accomplished that it said it would

3. Key issues or problems that need resolution

4. Decisions or resources the unit needs from senior management

5. Performance to objectives, when relevant

The act of producing a quarterly report can itself spur the unit manager to keep a close eye on the progress of implementation. It can also help keep upper management in the implementation loop (see "Don't Tempt People to Sweep Problems Under the Rug"). (Note: The appendix contains a handy project progress review worksheet. Consider using it as you develop progress reports for your strategy

---

Don't Tempt People to Sweep Problems Under the Rug

Some executives make it very clear that they don't want to hear any bad news. They tell their direct reports, "I want this done right and done on time. I don't want you coming in here telling me that you have a problem. If you have a problem, fix it. If you can't fix it, I'll find someone who can."

This attitude may create a "no-nonsense" image for the executive, but it can drive problems underground. Direct reports who cannot solve problems on their own—and who cannot find help—are likely to say, "Everything is fine, boss." Ever hopeful that some miracle will salvage the situation, they will continue hiding or minimizing problems until the very last minute, when denial is no longer possible. By that point, every opportunity to fix the problem will have been lost.

---

implementation. That worksheet is downloadable without charge from the Harvard Business Essentials series Web site: www.elearning .hbsp.org/businesstools.)

Informal Checks

Progress reviews are a formal and systematic way of identifying implementation problems. But informal checks made by curious and observant managers are every bit as valuable. Some senior executives make the mistake of compartmentalizing strategy initiatives into two distinctly separate activities: planning and doing. "We executives do all the strategic thinking and planning. Our people do the implementing." This attitude is a prescription for failure. Executives and managers need to stay close to the implementation action and physically look for problems. Instead of waiting for progress reports to arrive at their desks, they must routinely *see* and *be seen* on the front lines.

Progress reports are useful, but have a way of putting a positive spin on whatever is going on. The people who write them are often loath to admit problems—especially when there is some hope that they will eventually be overcome. Reports are no substitute for the evidence you can gather from simply watching people work and listening to what they have to say. Straightforward questioning of people in the operating units can reveal important information you might not find in progress reports. "How are things going?" "Are you getting the resources you need to reach your goals?" "What is blocking progress?" "How could I help you and your coworkers?"

For the senior manager or executive, asking questions costs very little, but can uncover hidden problems. Being seen is equally useful. Showing up, participating in team meetings, lending a hand with some of the more challenging tasks, and other forms of personal involvement provide tangible evidence that what employees are doing is important—"so important that the bosses come down here and help us get the job done." Showing up also provides senior managers with opportunities to reiterate what the strategy is, why it is important, and how everyone will benefit from its success.

Common Causes of Implementation Failure

Even the most carefully thought-out action plans can be derailed. Here are a few of the common causes:

PLANS ARE EXPANDED. During the execution of action plans, a project may increase in scope. For example, a product development group might decide to add features to a new product or to develop additional add-on products. Spending time on additional features and products cuts into the resources intended to carry out the original plan.

Antidote: Take all requests for plan expansion to the executive in charge of implementation. Explain how these requests will impact your implementation action plan and what additional time and resources will be needed to keep the plan on track. That person will have the authority to either deny the expansion request or give you the resources you need. Outsourcing certain parts of the action plan may be a feasible solution if the executive rules that plan expansion is essential.

PLANS ARE TRIMMED. A project may be cut back during implementation. This might be done to reduce costs or speed up implementation. While such measures might save money and time, they may also cause an action plan to fall short of achieving its original objectives.

Antidote: Again, a plan change of this nature should be adjudicated at the top. If the plan is being trimmed to save time, examine the reasoning that went into the original deadline. If the CEO said, "Get this job done by the end of the calendar year," that might have been a very arbitrary deadline. Is there anything special about the end of the year? Would the company's strategy be imperiled if the implementation period were lengthened by a few months? Once you have the answers to those questions, implementation leaders should determine if a trimmed-down plan finished on time is of greater value than the original plan finished somewhat later.

RESOURCES ARE INADEQUATE. Employees may not be given adequate time to work on strategic initiatives because of their regular duties. This may be a result of inaccurate resource estimates, an increase in project scope, or competing priorities. Whatever the cause, this truth remains: If everyone takes on too much work, resources will be strained.

Antidote: Be flexible and maintain a reserve. When they commit their troops to battle, experienced military commanders do so with the assumption that the clash will produce unforeseen dangers and opportunities. They hold a force in reserve to respond to these developments. A strategy implementation project is similar. It's impossible to foresee with certainty what resources a project will require and what problems will develop. Consequently, managers should build flexibility into their plans and hold some additional funds, equipment, or people in reserve. In a word: Be prepared for resource shortfalls.

INTERLOCKS FAIL. A group that your unit depends on for a deliverable or collaboration may alter its plans and therefore fail to fulfill its obligations to you. In many cases this occurs because that group's manager has failed to free up necessary resources or has other priorities. In other cases, interlocks were overlooked during the action-planning stage.

Collaboration between units is always an issue, unless these units routinely work together. Causes of collaboration problems include the following:

- Poor communication ("We don't know what they want from us.")

- Misalignment of goals or priorities

- Antagonism between unit managers

- Different working styles (e.g., one unit is entrepreneurial; the other is bureaucratic)

- Lack of incentives for collaboration

Antidote: Communication. Higher management should state in unambiguous terms: "This strategy implementation is a key goal for the company. I expect you to work together to make it succeed." Also, communication will not be a problem if interlock units participate fully in developing the implementation action plans.

CHANGE IS RESISTED. A new strategy produces more than a change in a company's competitive stance; it also upsets the status quo inside the organization, producing change resisters. "The reformer has enemies in all those who profit by the old order," Machiavelli warned his readers. And what held true in sixteenth-century Italy remains true today. Some people clearly enjoy advantages that they think will be threatened by change. They may perceive change as endangering their livelihoods, their perks, their workplace social arrangements, or their status in the organization. Others know that their specialized skills will be rendered less valuable. For example, when a supplier of automotive hydraulic steering systems switched to electronic steering technology in the late 1990s, long-term employees with expertise in hoses, valves, and fluids were suddenly less important. The know-how they had developed over long careers was suddenly less valuable to the company, displaced by the electrical engineering skills the company was actively recruiting.

Any time people perceive themselves as losers in a change initiative, expect resistance. Resistance may be passive, in the form of noncommitment to goals, or active, in the form of direct opposition or subversion. How will you deal with that resistance?

Antidote: Identify potential resisters and redirect their angst. Here's how to start:

- Determine who has something to lose in your company's strategy change, and communicate the "why" of change to them. Explain the urgency of moving away from established routines or arrangements.

- Emphasize the benefits of the new strategy to potential resisters. Those benefits might be greater future job security, higher pay, and so forth. There's no guarantee that these benefits of change will exceed the losses for these individuals. However, explaining the benefits will help shift their focus from negatives to positives.

- Help resisters find new roles—roles that represent genuine contributions *and* mitigate their losses.

- Empower resisters. Many people resist change because it represents a loss of control over their daily lives. Return some of that control by making them active partners in the strategy implementation program.

If these interventions fail, move resisters out of your unit. You cannot afford to let a few disgruntled individuals subvert the progress of the entire group. But don't make them "walk the plank." Do what you can to relocate them to positions where their particular skills can be better used. That's what the innovator of electronic steering systems did. That company still had plenty of business supplying hydraulic systems to car and truck manufacturers, so it employed its hydraulic specialists in those units even as it hired electronic engineers for its expanding new business.

Develop Contingency Plans to Handle Potential Setbacks

Like every strategic plan, every implementation plan contains the risk that something unforeseen or unforeseeable will come along and cause delay or derailment. Contingency plans should be developed for these potential problems. A *contingency plan* is a course of action prepared in advance of a potential problem; it answers the question, "If X happens, how could we respond in a way that would neutralize or minimize the damage?" Here are two examples of project contingency plans:

- The Acme Company set up a two-year project to modernize its manufacturing facilities. Senior management regarded the two-year deadline as extremely important. Recognizing the real risk that the deadline might not be met, the sponsor agreed to set up a reserve fund that could be used to hire outside help if the project fell behind schedule. This contingency plan included a monthly progress review and a provision that falling three or more weeks behind schedule would trigger release of the reserve funds.

- TechnoWhiz, Inc. was banking on its software project team to develop a new version of its integrated office application suite, one that would include all the bells and whistles, and seamless linkages to the Internet. Not wanting to miss the announced release date and its expensive marketing roll-out, the team developed a contingency plan for dealing with any unfinished elements of the program. That plan was clear: Any new elements not ready for the official release date would be packaged as a downloadable "add-on" to be made available at a later date to all registered users of the new version. Staffing for the development of this add-on was planned in advance, with budgeting conditional on the amount of work needed.

The real benefit of a contingency plan is that it prepares people to deal with an adverse situation. When disaster strikes, managers and employees don't have to spend weeks trying to figure out what they should do or how they will find the funds to deal with a new situation.

Has your unit identified the risks in its implementation plan? Has it developed contingency plans for dealing with them? ("Make Someone Responsible for Each Serious Risk" offers another angle on making implementation plans work.)

Keeping implementation on track lacks the fun of the mental game of strategy creation. And though strategy makers get most of the credit when a new strategy succeeds, the executives and lower-ranking managers who keep implementation on course have the most important job because, in the end, even the most brilliant strategy isn't worth much if it is poorly implemented.

Make Someone Responsible for Each Serious Risk

Just as every task in an action plan should have an "owner," every serious risk should be someone's responsibility. That person should monitor the assigned risk, sound the alarm if the risk appears to be moving from potential problem to real problem, and be prepared to deal with the consequences.

Summing Up

- Strategy failures are often a product of poor implementation.

- You can sense deviations from action plans through these mechanisms: performance metrics; periodic progress reviews; anecdotal reports; direct observation.

- Weekly or monthly progress reviews are the best mechanisms for catching implementation problems before they grow into a major impediment to success.

- If you are the boss, don't create a climate in which people are afraid to report implementation problems in a timely way.

- Executives and managers should not wait for progress reports, but should be out on the front lines of implementation, observing and asking questions.

- Common causes of implementation failures include plan expansions, plans that are trimmed, inadequate resources, interlock failures, and resistance by employees who see themselves as losers under the new strategy.

- Every implementation plan contains risks—some unforeseeable. Create a contingency plan for every serious risk.

- Make someone responsible for the management of every serious risk.

8

The People Side of Implementation

Getting the Right People on Board

Key Topics Covered in This Chapter

- *How to enlist the support and involvement of key people in a change initiative*

- *Supporting the plan with consistent behaviors*

- *Enabling structures (i.e., training, pilot programs, and a reward system)*

- *Ways to celebrate milestones*

- *The importance of relentless communication*

T HE PREVIOUS TWO chapters could give the impression that strategy implementation is a mechanical process: Just develop a blueprint of action steps, tell employees to execute those steps, and check periodically for compliance and progress. The reality is that people are the most important part of implementation, and harnessing their energy and commitment to strategic change is often management's greatest challenge. People have to feel that they've had something to say about the plans they are told to implement. They must know that success is important. They must be motivated to do the right things well. And they must see real incentives for their hard work.

The record shows that implementation rarely proceeds smoothly. In some cases, external factors upset schedules or divert the attention of management. Technical glitches hamstring progress. But people problems are more often the cause of implementation problems. People make mistakes. Key employees quit or are transferred. Different groups forget to communicate with each other. Untrained people are assigned to jobs they cannot handle. Managers alienate the employees charged with critical action steps. This chapter addresses the people side of implementation and aims to steer you clear of problems.

Enlist the Support and Involvement of Key People

Your implementation will go more smoothly if it has the backing and involvement of key people—and not just the CEO and his or her court. It goes without saying that top-level involvement is essential. But it is also necessary to enlist the support of managers and employees whom others respect: individuals with proven technical skills, people with access to vital resources, and the informal leaders to whom people naturally turn for direction and advice when they encounter obstacles. How can you identify these people? Authors Michael Tushman and Charles O'Reilly offer this advice:

> *To determine who these key individuals are and what their responses to the change might be, ask: Who has the power to make or break the change? Who controls critical resources or expertise? Then think through how the change will likely affect each of these individuals and how each is likely to react toward the change. Who will gain or lose something? . . . Are there blocs of individuals likely to mobilize against or in support of the change effort?*[1]

Enlisting support entails building an effective team of change makers who can work in unison toward stated goals. But how can you be sure you've picked the right people for the team? Here's a set of questions that will help you know if your team has the right stuff:[2]

- Are enough of your company's key players (people in relevant positions of power) members of the team?

- Do members of the team have the relevant expertise to do the job and make intelligent decisions?

- Does the team include the needed range of perspectives and disciplines to do the job and make intelligent decisions?

- Does the team include people with sufficient credibility so that employees and management will treat its decisions seriously?

- Does the team include true leaders?

- Are the team members capable of forgoing their personal interests in favor of the larger organizational goal?

If you answered "yes" to most of these questions, the team guiding the implementation effort is strong and in a good position to succeed. If you said "no" to any questions, it might be a good idea to revisit your team choices. (For more on selecting team members, see "Tips on Who Should *Not* Be on the Team.")

Tips on Who Should Not *Be on the Team*

In his book on *Leading Change,* John Kotter recommends that you keep three types of people off your team:[a]

1. **People with big egos.** Big egos, says Kotter, fill the room, leaving little or no space for anybody else to participate or contribute. People with big egos don't always understand their own limitations and how those limitations can be complemented by the strength of others.

2. **Snakes.** Kotter describes a "snake" as the kind of person who secretly poisons relationships between team members. "A snake is an expert at telling Sally something about Fred and Fred something about Sally that undermines Sally and Fred's relationship."

3. **Reluctant players.** These are people who lack either the time or enthusiasm to provide energy to the team. Be wary of including these people on your team. Keeping them off may be difficult, however, since some reluctant players may have the expertise and/or organizational power you need.

Implementing a new strategy is difficult enough without having these people on your team.

[a] John F. Kotter, *Leading Change* (Boston: Harvard Business School Press, 1996), 59–61.

Support the Plan with Consistent
Behaviors and Messages

Once the need for change has been articulated convincingly and broad support has been enlisted, support must be maintained through a set of consistent behaviors and messages. Inconsistency in either will send a damaging signal—that management is either not serious about implementing the new strategy or unwilling to do its part.

Consider this example: Not many years ago, one of the American Big Three automakers underwent a painful strategic restructuring. Everyone was asked to sacrifice by giving up benefits today in order to achieve greater competitiveness, job security, and prosperity tomorrow. Thousands of middle managers were laid off and the company's union was asked to forgo pay and benefit increases. Because the company had made a convincing case for change, people got the message and tightened their belts; even the unions pitched in. Within months, however, senior management awarded itself and other key people substantial bonuses and pay increases. Once that inconsistent behavior became public, the bonds of trust between management and the rank and file—and union leaders—evaporated. Collaboration turned to open hostility that simmered for nearly ten years.

At about the same time, a company in another industry was likewise supporting a belt-tightening and restructuring program. But this one did so with highly visible and consistent behaviors from leaders. Its CEO set the pace by selling the corporation's three jets and taking commercial flights on his travels—in coach class to boot. And no more limos to meet him at the airport. "I don't mind taking a cab," he told the business press. "They can get me to where I'm going just as fast." The company's other traveling executives followed the lead of their boss. People noticed.

Which of these companies do you suppose was more successful in building support for its change program?

SQA, Herman Miller's successful low-cost office furniture unit mentioned in an earlier chapter, also used a consistent set of messages to support its strategy of on-time, accurate fulfillment of orders.

Everyone understood that this was the unit's key measure of success. So SQA managers came up with several ways to reinforce that message. For example, every morning they posted the previous day's percentage of on-time orders at every entrance to the plant. It was impossible to enter or leave without knowing these figures. They also added the latest on-time order statistic to every internal e-mail message. "Yesterday's percentage of on-time accurately filled orders was 99.2 percent." The vice president of operations even adopted the practice of randomly asking employees if they knew the previous day's performance score. A correct answer was rewarded with either a crisp $100 bill or a day off with full pay.

What messages or behaviors would be consistent with the implementation program at your company?

Develop Enabling Structures

Enabling structures are the activities and programs that underpin successful implementation and are a critical part of the overall plan. Such structures include pilot programs, training, and reward systems.

Pilot programs give people opportunities to grapple with implementation and its problems on a smaller, more manageable scale. They are test beds in which implementers can experiment with and de-bug initiatives before rolling them out more broadly. These programs can be valuable proving grounds, since it's almost always easier and less risky to change a single department than an entire company.

Training programs can hold equal value. Motorola and General Electric developed formal training programs that served as key enablers for the quality strategies adopted by these companies. Xerox did the same when it set up its companywide benchmarking program in the mid-1980s. Every Xerox employee received a copy of "the little yellow book," as they called the company's how-to manual on benchmarking methods, and skilled trainers were placed in almost every operating unit of the company.

Reward systems also play an enabling role. People generally adopt behaviors that produce rewards, and abandon those that are not rewarded. Thus, if your action plan asks people to either work harder, work smarter, or work in new ways, your reward system must be aligned with those desired behaviors. The details and pitfalls of crafting incentive programs are complex and situationally determined. Thus, they need to be crafted within the context of each organization. Here are some questions to ask as you consider setting up enabling structures:

- Can you find a place for pilot programs in your strategy implementation?

- What training, if any, is appropriate before you move forward with action plans?

- Is employee behavior aligned with action plans through rewards?

Celebrate Milestones

Strategy implementation can be a long and frustrating road. People are bound to grow tired or lose interest if positive actions are not taken to keep up their spirits and energy. You can keep people fired up if you identify milestones—even small ones—and celebrate them as they are achieved. (See "Tips for Celebrating Short-Term Wins.") Celebrating a series of short-term wins can:

- neutralize skepticism about the strategy and implementation efforts;

- provide evidence that peoples' sacrifices and hard work are paying off;

- help retain support;

- keep up the momentum; and

- boost morale.

Tips for Celebrating Short-Term Wins

Here are just a few ideas for celebrating short-term wins and keeping your team pumped up:

• Treat implementers to a catered lunch—and bring in an outside speaker who can talk about his or her company's success in doing something similar.

• Take the afternoon off for a softball game.

• Recognize the work of exceptional contributors.

Do something grander for major successes. For example, when you've successful reached the midpoint of the initiative, host a dinner with the CEO as guest and keynote speaker. Whatever you do, it is very important to mark passages along the road toward complete implementation.

There is a fine line between celebrating a successful milestone and making a premature declaration of victory. Crossing that line could dissipate the sense of urgency you need to keep people motivated and moving on toward future hurdles. John Kotter, who lists "declaring victory too soon" among the reasons that transformation efforts fail, says that both change initiators and change resisters have reasons for making this mistake. "In their enthusiasm over a clear sign of progress," he writes, "the initiators go overboard. They are then joined by [resisters], who are quick to point out any opportunity to stop change. . . . [The resisters] point to the victory as a sign that the war has been won and the troops should be sent home."[3] Catastrophe follows if the weary troops accept this argument and go back to their usual activities.

So instead of declaring victory, use the credibility and momentum gained from your short-term win to muster an attack on the next milestone.

Communicate Relentlessly

Communication is the most important implementation tool available to management. They must use communication to make clear:

- what the strategy is;

- why the strategy is important;

- how effective implementation will benefit the company and employees; and

- what role each person will play in implementing the strategy.

These four points should form the core of the CEO's pep talk to managers and employees. And they should be the core of every manager's communication to direct reports and their subordinates.

Communication is an effective tool for motivating employees, for overcoming resistance, for preparing people for the pluses and minuses of change, and for giving employees a personal stake in strategy implementation. Effective communication can set the tone for the difficult work ahead and is critical to implementation from the very start. But don't rely on a single Big Bang announcement to keep employees in line with the effort. Communication must be ongoing. Here are some tips for communicating during a change effort:[4]

1. **Specify the nature of the new strategy and the results you aim for.** Slogans, themes, and phrases don't define what the strategy is expected to achieve. Communicate specific information about how the new strategy will affect customer satisfaction, quality, market share or sales, or productivity.

2. **Explain why.** Employees are often left in the dark about the business reasons behind a strategy change. You may have spent lots of time studying the problem and digging out the facts, but your coworkers aren't privy to that information. In addition, share with employees the various options available and why one is better than the others.

3. **Explain the scope of the strategy change, even if it contains bad news.** Some people will be more affected than others. And that leads to lots of fear-generating speculation. Fear and uncertainty can paralyze a company. You can short-circuit fear and uncertainty with the facts. But don't sugarcoat them. If people will be laid off, be up-front about it. If others will need training, say so. Also explain the things that will *not* change. This will help anchor people.

4. **Develop a graphic representation of the implementation action plan that people can understand and hold in their heads.** It might be a flow chart of what must happen, or a graphic image of what the changed enterprise will look like. Whatever it is, keep it clear, simple, and memorable.

5. **Predict the negative aspects of implementation.** There are bound to be negatives, and people should anticipate them. These include hard work, changes in assignments, and frustrating problems. If you prepare people for these eventualities, they will take them in stride.

6. **Explain the criteria for success and how it will be measured.** Define success clearly, and devise metrics for progress toward it. These are part of your action plan. If you fail to establish clear measures for what you aim to accomplish, how will people know if they are moving forward or in the right direction? Measure progress as you move forward—and then communicate that progress.

7. **Explain how people will be rewarded for success.** As stated elsewhere, people need incentives for the added work and disruptions that change requires. Be very clear about how individuals will be rewarded for progress toward implementation goals.

8. **Repeat, repeat, and repeat the purpose of change and actions planned.** If the initial announcement doesn't generate ques-

tions, do not assume that employees accept the need for change—they may simply be surprised, puzzled, or shocked. So follow up your initial announcement meeting with another meeting. Follow this with communications that address individual aspects of the change project.

9. **Use a diverse set of communication styles.** Some people are most receptive to the printed word, or to flow charts. Others respond best to stand-up presentations. Since every audience contains people with different learning styles, provide a mix of mediums—a dedicated newsletter, events, e-mails, and stand-up presentations—to keep people informed, involved, and keyed up. These communications should be honest about successes and failures. If people lose trust in what they are hearing, they will tune you out.

10. **Make communication a two-way proposition.** Remember that strategy implementation is a shared enterprise. So spend at least as much time listening as telling. Your attention to this point will help keep others involved and motivated. Leaders need feedback, and the hardworking implementers need opportunities to share their learning and their concerns with leaders who listen.

11. **Be consistent.** If you're the boss, people will have their eyes on you. They will listen to your words, but will also look for inconsistencies between your words and what you communicate through body language and behavior. Do you speak and act with genuine enthusiasm? Do your tone and manner signal confidence in the implementation project, or do you appear to be going through the motions? Try to see yourself as others see you.

In the end, the people side of implementation should be the most important concern of managers. Without employee commitment and hard work, action plans are wasted paper.

Summing Up

- Get the right people involved in implementation. These should include individuals with proven technical skills, people with access to vital resources, and the informal leaders to whom people naturally turn for direction and advice when they encounter obstacles.

- Keep people with big egos, too little time, and no enthusiasm, as well as troublemakers, off the implementation team.

- Be consistent in your behavior and messages. Don't ask people to make sacrifices on behalf of the new strategy if you, as a leader, are not willing to make them yourself.

- Successful implementation is supported by enabling structures: pilot programs, training, and reward systems.

- Celebrate as you achieve important milestones. Doing so will help maintain momentum, support, and morale.

- Don't declare victory too early.

- Keep up a steady level of communication. Remind people about the nature of the strategy, why it's important, how it will benefit employees and the company, and the roles they are expected to play.

- Be open to communication from others.

Strategy as Work–in–Progress

Keep Looking Ahead

Key Topics Covered in This Chapter

- *Why executives must evaluate strategy effectiveness*

- *Using financial ratios, the balanced scorecard, and market analysis to measure strategy effectiveness*

- *Warning signs of strategy peril*

- *Leading strategic change*

I F YOU CREATE a winning strategy and implement it well, you might cruise along for years without problems. But no strategy is effective forever. Something in the external environment eventually changes, rendering your current strategy ineffective or unprofitable. It is difficult to think of an industry in which this has not happened. As Clayton Christensen reminded readers of the *Harvard Business Review* several years ago:

> It is sobering to review yesterday's list of great corporate strategies: Ford's mass production of standard automobiles; General Motors' adoption of vertical integration and design of cars tailored to the preferences of customers in each tier of the market; Xerox's strategy of selling copies rather than copiers; and Sears's sales of reliable, reasonably priced merchandise through stores located in growing suburbs. Guided by brilliant strategies, these companies rose to prominence. Yet when conditions in their competitive environments changed, each found it extraordinarily difficult to change strategic direction.[1]

Many management teams, unfortunately, are unable (or unwilling) to recognize when their strategies have become less potent—if not obsolete. Either because of myopia or hubris they fail to understand how the external environment is changing and do not come to grips with that change through an altered strategy. Strategy *re*-creation, then, is an ongoing requirement of good management. It is, to quote Michael Porter, "a process of perceiving new positions that woo customers from established positions or draw new customers into the market."[2]

This chapter explains how managers can assess the effectiveness of their current strategies and recognize warning signs that they are losing the power to capture and satisfy customers. The temporary nature of successful strategy should caution every leader to continually scan the external environment for threats and new opportunities, as described earlier in this book. What they learn through that scanning should inform their thinking about whether it's time to alter or replace the current strategy.

How Well Is Your Strategy Working?

The strategy model presented in the introduction to this book (figure I-1) indicated feedback loops from the performance measurement piece of the model back to the very beginning of the strategy creation process. Measurement tells leaders how well their strategy and its implementation are working. Substandard measures should spur them to look once again to the external environment for threats and opportunities and to the internal environment for existing capabilities. This section profiles three approaches to strategy performance measurement: financial analysis, the balanced scorecard, and market analysis.

Financial Analysis

The proof of a strategy's power or weakness is reflected in a company's financial statements: particularly its balance sheet and income statement. Examination of the profitability ratios based on financial statement figures yields further insight about the strategy's effectiveness.

FINANCIAL STATEMENTS. The balance sheet describes assets owned by the business and how those assets are financed—with the funds of creditors (liabilities) and the equity of owners. The income statement (sometimes referred to as the profit and loss statement) indicates the cumulative results of operations over a specified period. By comparing these results from one year to the next, is possible to gauge the effectiveness of both strategy and its implementation through operations—though separating the two is often difficult. Consider the case of Amalgamated Hat Rack Company, whose multi-period income statement is represented in table 9-1. Amalgamated's retail sales demonstrate steady growth even as its operating expenses

TABLE 9-1

Amalgamated Hat Rack Multiperiod Income Statement

| | FOR THE PERIOD ENDING DECEMBER 31 | | | |
	2004	2003	2002	2001
Retail Sales	$2,200,000	$2,000,000	$1,720,000	$1,500,000
Corporate Sales	$1,000,000	$1,000,000	$1,100,000	$1,200,000
Total Sales Revenue	$3,200,000	$3,000,000	$2,820,000	$2,700,000
Less: Cost of Goods Sold	$1,600,000	$1,550,000	$1,400,000	$1,300,000
Gross Profit	$1,600,000	$1,450,000	$1,420,000	$1,400,000
Less: Operating Expenses	$800,000	$810,000	$812,000	$805,000
Depreciation Expense	$42,500	$44,500	$45,500	$42,500
Earnings before Interest and Taxes	$757,500	$595,500	$562,500	$552,500
Less: Interest Expense	$110,000	$110,000	$150,000	$150,000
Earnings before Income Tax	$647,500	$485,500	$412,500	$402,500
Less: Income Tax	$300,000	$194,200	$165,000	$161,000
Net Income	$347,500	$291,300	$247,500	$241,500

Source: Harvard Business Essentials: Finance for Managers (Boston: Harvard Business School Press, 2002), 15.

have been held in check. Something is going well here. The company's corporate sales, however, are flagging from one year to the next. If corporate sales is an important piece of Amalgamated's strategy, then something is going wrong, either with the strategy or its execution. This piece of quantitative information should signal management to look closely at the problem.

Managers can also gain insights by examining the ratios of key figures drawn from the balance sheet and income statement. Ratios help an analyst or decision maker piece together a story about where an organization has come from, its current condition, and its possible future. In most cases, the story told by these ratios is incomplete, but it's a start.

PROFITABILITY RATIOS. Profitability ratios associate the amount of income earned with the resources used to generate it. Barring ineptness in operational implementation, the firm's strategy should produce as much profit as possible from a given amount of resources. The profitability ratios to remember are return on assets (ROA); return on equity (ROE); return on investment (ROI); and operating margin, or earnings before interest and taxes (EBIT).

Return on assets relates net income to the company's total asset base and is figured as follows:

ROA = Net Income/Total Assets

ROA relates net income to the investment in all the financial resources at the command of management. It is a useful measure of effective resource utilization without regard to how those resources were obtained or financed—a factor that shouldn't be considered in examining the effectiveness of strategy.

Return on equity relates net income to the financial resources invested by shareholders. It is a measure of how efficiently the shareholders' stake in the business has been used. ROE is calculated as follows:

ROE = Net Income/Shareholders' Equity

The term "return on investment" is often used in business discussions that involve profitability. For example, expressions like "We aim for an ROI of 12 percent" are common. Unfortunately, there is no standard definition of ROI, since "investment" may be construed from many perspectives. Investment might represent the assets committed to a particular activity, the shareholders' equity involved, or invested assets minus any liabilities generated by a company's taking on a project. ROI might also refer to the internal rate of return, a very specific calculation of return. So, when someone uses the term "return on investment," *always* request a clarification. Ask, "How are you calculating investment?"

The earnings-before-interest-and-taxes margin, more generally known as the *operating margin,* is used by many to gauge the profitability of a company's operating activities. The operating margin ignores the interest expenses and taxes over which current management may have no control, thus giving a clearer indicator of management performance. To calculate the operating margin, use this formula:

Operating Margin = EBIT/Net Sales

None of these ratios is a sure indicator of the strength or weakness of one's strategy since each reflects both the strategy *and* its execution. Nevertheless, ratios that are weaker than those of peer companies, or ratios that are growing weaker from one year to the next, should set off alarm bells in the executive suite and encourage senior management to investigate the causes. Is it the strategy, or is the strategy being poorly executed?

From Financial Measures to a Balanced Scorecard

Financial ratios tell the tale of business performance, and generations of businesspeople have used them to manage their operations. But financial ratios aren't buttons we can push to make things happen—instead, they are outcomes of dozens of other activities. And they are backward-looking, the products of past activities. Worse, traditional measures can send the wrong signals. For instance, profit measures that look very good this year may be the result of dramatic cuts in new-product development and reductions in employee training. On the surface, current high profitability can make the state of affairs look rosy, but cuts in project development and training jeopardize tomorrow's profits. Nor do financial ratios directly measure things such as customer satisfaction and organizational learning, which assure long-term profitability.

Frustrated by the inadequacies of traditional performance measurement systems, some managers have shifted their focus to the operational activities that produce them. These managers follow the motto "Make operational improvements, and the performance numbers will follow." But which improvements are the most important? Which are the true drivers of long-term, bottom-line performance? To answer these questions, Harvard Business School professor Robert Kaplan and his associate David Norton conducted research on a number of companies with leading-edge measures of performance. From this research, they developed what they call a *balanced scorecard*, a new performance measurement system that gives top managers a more comprehensive view of the business. The balanced scorecard includes financial measures that indicate the results of past actions. And it complements those financial measures with three sets of operational measures that relate directly to customer satisfaction, internal processes, and the organization's ability to learn and improve—the activities that drive future financial performance. In this sense the scorecard assesses both the company's strategy and its operational implementation.

Kaplan and Norton have compared the balanced scorecard to the dials and indicators in an airplane cockpit:

> *For the complex task of navigating and flying an airplane, pilots need detailed information about many aspects of the flight. They need information on fuel, air speed, altitude, bearing, destination, and other indicators that summarize the current and predicted environment. Reliance on one instrument can be fatal. Similarly, the complexity of managing an organization today requires that managers be able to view performance in several areas simultaneously.*[3]

Kaplan and Norton's balanced scorecard uses four perspectives to link performance measures and to galvanize managerial action.

Collectively, these perspectives give top management timely answers to four key questions:

- How do customers see us? (the customer perspective)

- What must we do to excel? (the internal perspective)

- Can we continue to improve and create value? (the innovation and learning perspective)

- How do we look to our shareholders? (the financial perspective)

Figure 9-1 indicates the linkages between the four perspectives. The advantage of the balanced scorecard over traditional measures is that three of the four perspectives (customer, innovation and learning, and internal) are more than results—they are levers that managers can manipulate to improve future results. For example, if the customer perspective indicator is in decline, management has a fairly clear idea where to intervene. Used together, the balanced scorecard and traditional ratio analysis can help managers understand the effectiveness of their strategy *and* identify areas where implementation needs work.

Market Analysis

Not too many years ago, a major publisher of college textbooks seemed pleased with its results. Revenue from sales was going up year after year, faster than expenses. There seemed like plenty of bonus money to go around—to shareholders, company managers, and the sales force. Only two disturbing facts intruded on this happy picture. First, the company's unit sales were flat, and had been so for three years in a row. Revenue growth was simply the product of the company's ability to increase its prices; a tactic that surely would not work forever. Second, revenues were dependent on the continued vitality of 5 books. Although the publisher actively promoted 180 current titles, these 5 accounted for 38 percent of total revenue. And each of them had been in the market for over fifteen years. Not one of the many other books this publisher had introduced during that

FIGURE 9-1

The Balanced Scorecard Links Performance Measures

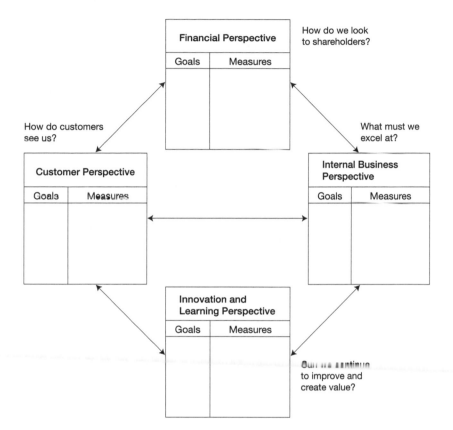

Source: Robert S. Kaplan and David P. Norton, "The Balanced Scorecard," *Harvard Business Review*, (January–February 1992), 72.

fifteen-year period had even come close to establishing a strong position in the market.

On the surface, this publisher's strategy appeared to be working. But market analysis revealed that it was simply treading water—going nowhere and being kept afloat by a handful of aging products Although the sales force was earning annual bonuses for regularly hitting its expanding revenue quotas, it was making no gains in the marketplace. And though the publisher's editors were developing and releasing new books every year, the company was living off past successes. Clearly, this company needed to examine its strategy through market analysis and find what was going wrong.

Market analysis is a big subject, too big to cover here. But you can capture many of its benefits if you focus your attention on just a few activities:

- **Customer acquisition.** Are you succeeding at acquiring new customers at an acceptable cost?

- **Customer profitability.** Are your current customers profitable to serve? Some companies focus solely on the number of new customers or accounts they corral, even though many of those customers are a drag on profits.

- **Customer retention.** Are you retaining your most valuable customers at a reasonable cost?

- **New products/service.** Are your new products/services successful and profitable?

- **Market share.** Are you gaining share in market segments that matter?

Negative answers to any questions on this short list should encourage you to reexamine you current business strategy.

Warning Signs

Strategic problems seldom appear overnight. But there are some early warning signs that something is going wrong. This section describes two of those signs and how you can respond.

The Appearance of New Competitors

Every successful and profitable strategy creates an unwelcome problem: It attracts competitors like bees to flowers. Unless hurdles are placed in their paths, the market will eventually become crowded, and competition and overcapacity will erode profits for everyone. And some of these new entrants may bring something different and superior to the market—for example, making their product or service more convenient to purchase.

Consider the example of the video rental stores that still populate many towns and urban neighborhoods. When movies were first made available on VHS cassettes (and Sony's "Beta" format), small-scale entrepreneurs set up rental shops to serve local markets. And many did very well. This was a fairly easy business to enter, requiring little in the way of technical know-how or capital. When the profitability of the initial vendors became evident, others flocked to the market, driving down prices and cutting back sales for almost all players. Eventually, the U.S. market for videos was taken over (as always seems to happen in the United States) by big national chains such as Blockbuster and Hollywood Hits. These operators had advantages of scale that small, local competitors couldn't match. Many of the original entrepreneurs went out of business.

The profitability of the big chains, in turn, has attracted innovative competitors, who are using pay-per-view, downloadable movies, and postal-based rentals to claim shares of the market.

If your business is successful, the reason for its success is that it provides something unique that customers value—or it sells/delivers its product or service in a manner they value (more quickly or conveniently). These qualities differentiate your company and give it a competitive advantage. The competitive advantage of that differentiation will disappear if new entrants begin doing the same thing.

Now ask yourself, "How easily can the unique qualities of our company or its products be copied by others?" If they can be easily copied, be prepared to share the market.

Market invasion by imitators is commonplace, and few market leaders can bar the door. Consider the case of Apple Computer and its popular iPod digital music player. Apple introduced the iPod in November 2001. It was not the first such device, but its design qualities and ability to store up to one thousand songs quickly made it a big success—the biggest for Apple since its Macintosh line of computers. The company sought to protect itself from direct imitators through a patented design and by farming out pieces of the iPod's manufacture to a mix of suppliers operating under nondisclosure agreements. As of this writing, Apple still has a major chunk of the market and is maintaining it through new releases of improved models. However, this has not stopped others, including such formidable vendors as Hewlett-Packard, Dell, Sony, and Samsung, from entering the market and carving out pieces for themselves.

There are several possible defenses against the invasion by rivals seeking to enter your market:

1. Deliberately erect barriers to entry. For example, a fast-food restaurant owner in a small town might buy up the pieces of real estate most attractive to a potential rival.

2. Don't maximize profits. If you are the market leader, seek market share dominance over profit maximization. This may sound like heresy, but it often makes sense. By establishing a pricing structure that produces only modest profits, fewer competitors will be drawn to your market.

3. Exploit the *experience curve* to establish yourself as the low-cost leader. This is particularly important in technology industries. If you can learn sooner and faster than competitors, you'll maintain a cost advantage; that advantage may be large enough to drive competitors out of the business and keep others away.

If none of these antidotes is feasible, you must alter your strategy in a way that differentiates your offer and gives it a competitive advantage.

The Appearance of a New Technology

The fates of many businesses hinge on their core technologies. Just as those technologies account for their success, the eclipse of those technologies results in their failure. For example, during the nineteenth century, harvesting ice from lakes and ponds was a huge business, particularly in New England. Ice harvested in the Boston area was packed by the Tucker Ice Company and its emulators into specially insulated vessels and shipped to Gulf coast cities, England, and as far away as India and China. It was a wonderfully profitable business until mechanical refrigeration technology was developed and disseminated around the world. Because of that innovation, the fortunes of the big ice companies gradually melted away.

The rise of digital photography provides a more current example. Ever since the late 1830s, imaging was based on the exposure of light to a film or a glass plate coated with photosensitive chemicals. That technology was progressively improved over the years. Kodak built an empire on chemical-based photography and did the most to advance the field, producing film, processing chemicals, and photographic paper for both the amateur and professional markets. It also marketed consumer cameras.

The first substantial threat to chemical-based photography appeared in the early 1980s when Sony, an electronics company, introduced a camera using digital technology. The rapid rise of digital photography—which makes the use of film, chemicals, and most papers obsolete—directly threatened Kodak and its manufacturing infrastructure. Worse, Kodak lacked superior competencies in digital imaging, at least initially. The universe of competitors also shifted dramatically. Kodak's main rival was no longer the film manufacturer Fuji; the explosive rise of digital imaging forced it into competition with Nikon, Canon, Leica, and other established camera makers. Even electronics firms such as Sony and Hewlett-Packard were in the game. By mid-2004, digital cameras had penetrated 40 percent of U.S. households and industry analysts were predicting another two years of rapid growth. Given this situation, Kodak had to undertake a huge strategic shift. To its credit, the company faced the facts and channeled its strategic resources into the technology of the future. How it will fare in the long run is anyone's guess.

Situations like Kodak's are common along fault lines created by technological progress. Business leaders must spot those disruptions in their very early stages and reformulate their strategies accordingly. When they spot them, they cannot bury their heads in the sand.

When faced with a new and disruptive technology, the impulse of many companies is to invest still further in the technologies that made them successful in the first place. This was observed when steamships challenged makers of sailing ships, when Edison's electric lighting systems challenged the gas-illumination companies in the late 1800s, and when jet engines challenged piston-driven aircraft engines in the late 1940s. In each case, the companies threatened by these innovations continued to invest in and marginally improve their mature technologies even as the new ones were becoming better and cheaper by the month.

The only antidotes to the invasion of new technologies are:

1. **Anticipate them.** New, strategy-wrecking technologies do not appear fully formed. They emerge slowly, often from different sources. In their formative periods they reveal themselves in scientific papers and are discussed at technical conferences. An alert company—one that continually scans the external environment—can often detect the new technologies long before they have developed to the point of being serious threats. This gives the company time to adapt or get on board. You can anticipate emerging technologies through policies that open the windows of your organization to the outer world: by sending R&D and marketing personnel to technical conferences, by setting up a scanning unit to review technical literature, and so forth.

2. **Go looking for trouble.** Ask this question: What could kill our business? Create a team of your brightest people and give them the job of developing a business strategy capable of penetrating your markets and stealing your current customers.

Leading Strategic Change

John Maynard Keynes, the British economist, was being pestered by a reporter. Why, the reporter asked, had Keynes recommended a shift from his former policy position? "When the facts change, I change my mind." Keynes asked the reporter, "What do you do, sir?" Leaders need to be as nimble in their thinking as Lord Keynes.

Holding fast to policies and strategies we've endorsed and supported for years is almost always easier than admitting that it's time to move on to something new. Consider the tragic case of U.S. President Lyndon Johnson, who committed American forces to years of bloody warfare in South Vietnam. Johnson's plan to defeat communist guerrillas and invading forces from the north was based on an untested "domino theory." If South Vietnam fell to the communists, according to that theory, all of Southeast Asia would likewise fall. As would the Philippines, and Japan, and who knew what else. As the toll on U.S. personnel and the nation's treasury mounted and support for the war withered, Johnson stayed the course. He clung to his policy despite substantial personal anguish and doubts, and despite growing evidence that the war was going badly. Through the worst of it, his administration would tell the public that "There is light at the end of the tunnel."

The fact that political and business leaders cling too long to strategies that have failed to achieve their objectives or outlived their usefulness should not surprise us. Our culture honors persistence, pressing forward in the face of adversity, and staying the course when more timid folk are ready to give up. But, sometimes, there is no light at the end of the tunnel, and moving onto another course is the wiser and braver action. That takes real leadership, which is a lot different from simply presiding over the status quo. The financial and other warning signs described in this chapter can help you know when it's time to move. Continual scanning of the external and internal environments can do the same.

Summing Up

- Even the most successful strategies do not last forever. Be alert to signals that it's time to rethink or recalibrate your current strategy.

- Financial analysis, the balanced scorecard, and market analysis can help you determine how well your strategy and its implementation are working.

- Profitability ratios—particularly return on assets, return on equity, and operating margin—are valuable indicators of strategy and implementation effectiveness.

- The weakness of traditional profitability ratios is that they are backward-looking. Nor do they directly measure the things such as customer satisfaction and organizational learning, which, in the long run, assure profitability. Many find the balanced scorecard approach to be a superior measure of company performance.

- The balanced scorecard rates a company on four dimensions: the customer, internal, innovation and learning, and financial perspectives.

- Market analysis should, at a minimum, examine company performance with respect to customer acquisition, customer profitability, customer retention, the success of new products and services, and market share.

- Warning signs that it's time to reexamine your strategy include the appearance of new competitors and the appearance of a new technology.

Useful Implementation Tools

This appendix contains three worksheets you may find useful. All the forms are adapted from Harvard ManageMentor®, an online product of Harvard Business School Publishing. The Project Progress Report form can be downloaded without charge from the Harvard Business Essentials series Web site: www.elearning.hbsp.org/businesstools. Readers can freely access this and other worksheets, checklists, and interactive tools found on that site.

1. **Worksheet for Conducting a SWOT Analysis (figure A-1).** The SWOT analysis, as described in chapters 1 and 2, is used by strategic planners to identify a company's strengths, weaknesses, opportunities, and threats. This worksheet can help you to be systematic in thinking about and evaluating these internal and external factors with respect to your company.

2. **Work Breakdown Structure (figure A-2).** The work breakdown structure is borrowed from the art and science of project management and can be useful in strategy implementation. You can use this worksheet to deconstruct large tasks into their component parts and then estimate the time needed to complete each.

3. **Project Progress Report (figure A-3).** Use this form to help assess progress, present this information to others, and think through next steps.

FIGURE A-1

Worksheet for Conducting a SWOT Analysis

Date of analysis: _____
What is being analyzed: **e.g., new product development** _____

Internal Analysis

List factors inherent to what is being analyzed.

Strengths	Ideas for building on these strengths
Weaknesses	**Ideas for reducing these weaknesses**

External Analysis

List factors external to what is being analyzed, such as customer needs or marketplace trends.

Opportunities	Ideas for investigating or taking advantage of these opportunities
Threats	**Ideas for minimizing or overcoming these threats**

Source: Harvard ManageMentor® on Implementing Strategy, adapted with permission.

FIGURE A-2

Work Breakdown Structure

Develop a Work Breakdown Structure (WBS) to ensure that you do not overlook a significant part of a complex activity or underestimate the time and money needed to complete the work. Use multiple pages as needed.

Describe the overall project:			
Major Task	**Level 1 Subtasks**	**Level 2 Subtasks**	**Level 2 Subtask Duration**
Total duration (hours/weeks/days)			
Major Task	**Level 1 Subtasks**	**Level 2 Subtasks**	**Level 2 Subtask Duration**
Total duration (hours/weeks/days)			

Source: Harvard ManageMentor® on Project Management, adapted with permission.

FIGURE A-3

Project Progress Report

Use this form to help assess progress, present this information to others, and think through next steps.

Project:	**Prepared by:**
For the period from:	**To:**

Current Status	
Key milestones for this period:	
Achieved (list)	Coming up next (list)
Key issues or problems:	
Resolved (list)	Need to be resolved (list)

Key decisions:			
Made (list)	Need to be made (list)	By whom	When

Budget status:

Implications
List changes in objectives, timeline/delivery dates, project scope, and resource allocation (including people and financial).

Next steps		
List the specific action steps that will be done to help move this project forward successfully. Put a name and date next to each step if possible.		
Step	Person responsible	Date

Comments:

Source: Harvard ManageMentor® on Project Management, adapted with permission.

Notes

Introduction

1. Carl von Clausewitz, *On War*, Volume 1 (London: Kegan Paul), 177.

2. Edward Mead Earle, ed., *Makers of Modern Strategy* (Princeton, NJ: Princeton University Press, 1943).

3. Kenneth Andrews, *The Concept of Corporate Strategy* (Homewood, IL: Richard D. Irwin, Inc., 1971).

4. Michael E. Porter, *Competitive Strategy* (New York: Free Press, 1980), xxiv.

5. Bruce Henderson, "The Origin of Strategy," *Harvard Business Review*, November–December 1989.

6. Michael E. Porter, "What Is Strategy?" *Harvard Business Review*, November–December 1996, 61–78.

7. Joan Magretta, "Why Business Models Matter," *Harvard Business Review*, May 2002, 86–92.

Chapter 1

1. Michael E. Porter, *Competitive Strategy* (New York: Free Press, 1980), 3.

2. George Day and David J. Reibstein, *Wharton on Dynamic Competitive Strategy* (New York: John Wiley & Sons, Inc., 1997), 23.

3. Michael E. Porter, "How Competitive Forces Shape Strategy," *Harvard Business Review*, March–April 1979, 113–145.

Chapter 2

1. James Surowiecki, *The Wisdom of Crowds* (New York: Doubleday, 2004), xvii.

2. The nine steps are adapted from Harvard ManageMentor® on Implementing Strategy, an online product of Harvard Business School Publishing.

Chapter 3

1. David Bovet and Joseph Martha, *Value Nets* (New York: John Wiley & Sons, Inc., 2000), 30.

2. For more on USAA, see Tom Teal, "Service Comes First: An Interview with USAA's Robert F. McDermott," *Harvard Business Review*, September–October 1991, 116–127.

3. Forrester Research, News Release, http://biz.yahoo.com/bw/040610/105021_1.html (accessed 10 June 2004).

4. Michael E. Porter, "What Is Strategy?" *Harvard Business Review*, November–December 1996, 61–78.

Chapter 4

1. Carl von Clausewitz, *On War*, Volume 1 (London: Kegan Paul).

2. David B. Yoffie and Mary Kwak, *Judo Strategy* (Boston: Harvard Business School Press, 2001), 3.

3. Ibid., 59–60.

4. Ibid., 14.

5. Jim Collins, "The Merger Mystery: Why Companies Cannot Buy Their Way to Greatness, *Time*, 29 November 2004, x.

Chapter 5

1. For the complete story, see David Bovet and Joseph Martha, *Value Nets* (New York: John Wiley & Sons, Inc., 2000), 169–182; and "Value Chain Report: Herman Miller Reinvests for Success," *Industry Week Value Chain,* December 12, 2000, www.iwvaluechain.com/Columns/columns.asp?/ColumnId-720 (accessed 28 January 2001).

2. Jeffrey Pfeffer, *The Human Equation* (Boston: Harvard Business School Press, 1998), xvi.

3. George Labovitz and Victor Rosansky, *The Power of Alignment* (New York: John Wiley & Sons, Inc, 1997), 35–36.

4. Dwight Gertz and João Baptista, *Grow To Be Great* (New York: Free Press, 1995), 154–155.

5. David J. Collis and Cynthia A. Montgomery, "Creating Corporate Advantage," *Harvard Business Review*, May–June 1998, 70–83.

6. Michael E. Porter, "What Is Strategy," *Harvard Business Review*, November–December 1996, 61–78.

7. Ibid., 70.

8. See About Us/McKnight Principles, 3M Company Web site, www.3M.com (accessed 5 October 2004).

Chapter 6

1. This chapter on action plans is adapted from Harvard ManageMentor® on Implementing Strategy, an online product of Harvard Business School Publishing.

Chapter 7

1. Sections of this chapter are adapted from Harvard ManageMentor® on Implementing Strategy, an online product of Harvard Business School Publishing.

2. Larry Bossidy and Ram Charan, *Execution: The Discipline of Getting Things Done* (New York: Crown Business, 2002), 15.

Chapter 8

1. Michael L. Tushman and Charles A. O'Reilly III, *Winning Through Innovation* (Boston: Harvard Business School Press, 1997), 190.

2. John Kotter, *Leading Change* (Boston: Harvard Business School Press, 1996).

3. John Kotter, "Leading Change: Why Transformation Efforts Fail," *Harvard Business Review*, March–April 1995, 66.

4. Adapted from Rebecca Saunders, "Communicating Change," *Harvard Management Communication Letter* (August 1999).

Chapter 9

1. Clayton M. Christensen, "Making Strategy: Learning by Doing," *Harvard Business Review*, November–December 1997, 141.

2. Michael E. Porter, "What Is Strategy?" *Harvard Business Review,* November–December 1996, 61–78.

3. Robert S. Kaplan and David P. Norton, "The Balanced Scorecard: Measures That Drive Performance," *Harvard Business Review,* January–February 1992. For a fuller discussion of the balanced scorecard and its implementation, see Robert S. Kaplan and David P. Norton, *The Balanced Scorecard* (Boston: Harvard Business School Press, 1996).

Glossary

ACTION PLAN A document that addresses strategic objectives and the steps required to achieve them.

ACTION STEPS The "who," "what," and "when" involved in carrying out a strategic initiative and achieving assigned goals. The sum of these action steps should complete the job.

ALIGNMENT For a business, a condition in which organizational structures, support systems, processes, human skills, resources, and incentives support strategic goals.

BALANCED SCORECARD A performance measurement system that includes financial measures and three sets of operational measures that relate directly to customer satisfaction, internal processes, and the company's ability to learn and improve—the activities that drive future financial performances.

BENCHMARKING An objective method for rating one's own activities against similar activities performed by organizations recognized for best practice. In addition to providing a method for self-evaluation, benchmarking aims to identify opportunities for process improvement.

BUSINESS MODEL A conceptual description of an enterprise's revenue sources, cost drivers, investment size, and success factors and how they work together.

COMPETITIVE ADVANTAGE A function of strategy that puts a firm in a better position than rivals to create economic value for customers.

CONTINGENCY PLAN A course of action prepared in advance of a potential problem; it answers this question: "If X happens, how can we respond in a way that will neutralize or minimize the damage?"

145

CORE COMPETENCY   A company's expertise or skills in key areas that directly produce superior performance.

CULTURE   A company's values, traditions, and operating style.

DIFFERENTIATION STRATEGY   A strategy in which a company deliberately sets its product or service apart from those of rivals in a qualitative way that customers value.

EXPERIENCE CURVE   A concept that holds that the cost of doing a repetitive task decreases by some percentage each time the cumulative volume of production doubles.

FOCUS STRATEGY   A business strategy built on the goal of serving a targeted market or set of customers extremely well.

HURDLE RATE   The minimum rate of return expected from new projects that require substantial capital investments. It is usually calculated as the enterprise's cost of capital plus some expectation of profit.

IMPLEMENTATION   The concrete measures that turn strategic intent into reality.

INTERLOCK   Points of cross-functional collaboration in pursuit of a goal. These might take the form of a task force team, cooperative individuals in departments who supply resources or advice, and so forth.

JUDO STRATEGY   As conceptualized by authors David Yoffie and Mary Kwak, strategic moves based on principles of movement, balance, and leverage.

KAIZEN   A philosophy of continuous process improvement that encourages everyone, at every level, to seek out ways to incrementally improve what they are doing.

LEAD USERS   Companies and individuals whose needs are far ahead of typical users.

MARKET SEGMENTATION   A technique for dividing a large heterogeneous market of customers into smaller segments with homogeneous features.

NETWORK EFFECT   A phenomenon is which the value of a product increases as more products are sold and the network of users increases.

OPERATING MARGIN A financial ratio used by many analysts to gauge the profitability of a company's operating activities. It is calculated as earnings before interest and taxes (EBIT) divided by net sales.

OPPORTUNITIES In SWOT analysis, the trends, forces, events, and ideas that a company or unit can capitalize on.

PRICE ELASTICITY OF DEMAND A quantitative measure of customer price sensitivity.

PROCESS REENGINEERING An improvement concept that aims for large breakthrough change—either through wholesale change or elimination of existing processes.

RETURN ON ASSETS (ROA) Relates net income to the company's total asset base and is calculated as net income divided by total assets.

RETURN ON EQUITY (ROE) Relates net income to the amount invested by shareholders (both initially and through retained earnings). It is a measure of the productivity of the shareholders' stake in the business and is calculated as net income divided by shareholders' equity.

SKUNK WORKS A team of people brought together in one place to generate an innovative solution or to solve a particular problem. In some cases, skunk works are sited in remote settings to keep team members focused on their mission, to minimize interference from the rest of the organization, or to maintain secrecy.

STRATEGY A plan that will differentiate the enterprise and give it a competitive advantage over rivals.

STRENGTHS In a SWOT analysis, the capabilities that enable a company or unit to perform well—capabilities that need to be leveraged.

SUBSTITUTE Any good or service that can fill the role of another. Two goods are considered substitutes whenever an increase in the price of one results in increased purchases of the other.

SWOT ANALYSIS Analysis that investigates the strengths, weaknesses, opportunities, and threats facing a company or operating unit.

THREATS In a SWOT analysis, the possible events or forces that a company or unit must plan for or mitigate.

WEAKNESSES In a SWOT analysis, the characteristics that prohibit a company or unit from performing well and need to be addressed.

WINNER–TAKE–ALL STRATEGY Same as *network effect strategy*.

WORK BREAKDOWN STRUCTURE A planning tool that deconstructs a project's goals into the many tasks and subtasks required to achieve it.

For Further Reading

Articles

Christensen, Clayton. "Making Strategy: Learning by Doing." *Harvard Business Review*, November–December 1997. Companies find it difficult to change strategy for many reasons, but one stands out: Strategic thinking is not a core managerial competence at most companies. Managers are unable to develop competence in strategic thinking because they do it so rarely. Harvard Business School professor Clayton Christensen helps managers develop a creative strategy and a proficiency in strategic decision making. This article presents a three-stage method executives can use to conceive and implement a creative and coherent strategy themselves. The process forces managers to dig deep in order to understand the forces affecting their business. This method is a useful tool for managers because it helps them link strategic thinking with operational planning—two activities that are often separate but are more effective when connected.

Collis, David J., and Cynthia A. Montgomery. "Competing on Resources." *Harvard Business Review*, July–August 1995. How do you create and sustain a profitable strategy? Many of the approaches to strategy championed in the past have focused managers' attention inward, urging them to build a unique set of resources and capabilities. In practice, however, notions like core competence have too often become a "feel-good" exercise that no one fails. These authors explain how a company's resources drive its performance in a dynamic competitive environment, and they propose a new framework that moves strategic thinking forward in two ways: (1) by laying out a pragmatic and rigorous set of market tests to determine whether a company's resources are truly valuable enough to serve as the basis for strategy, and (2) by integrating this market view of capabilities with earlier insights about competition and industry structure.

149

Collis, David J., and Cynthia A. Montgomery. "Creating Corporate Advantage." *Harvard Business Review*, May–June 1998. What differentiates truly great corporate strategies from the merely adequate? How can executives at the corporate level create tangible advantage for their business that makes the whole more than the sum of the parts? This article presents a comprehensive framework for value creation in the multibusiness company. It addresses the most fundamental questions of corporate strategy: What businesses should a company be in? How should it coordinate activities across businesses? What role should the corporate office play? How should the corporation measure and control performance?

Eisenhardt, Kathleen, and Donald Sull. "Strategy as Simple Rules." *Harvard Business Review*, January 2001. The success of Yahoo!, eBay, and other companies that have become adept at morphing to meet the demands of changing markets can't be explained using traditional thinking about competitive strategy. These companies have succeeded by pursuing constantly evolving strategies in market spaces that were considered unattractive according to traditional measures. In this article—the third in an HBR series by Eisenhardt and Sull on strategy in the new economy—the authors ask, What are the sources of competitive advantage in high-velocity markets? The secret, they say, is strategy as simple rules. The companies know that the greatest opportunities for competitive advantage lie in market confusion, but they recognize the need for a few crucial strategic processes and a few simple rules. In traditional strategy, advantage comes from exploiting resources or stable market positions. In strategy as simple rules, advantage comes from successfully seizing fleeting opportunities. Key strategic processes, such as product innovation, partnering, or spinout creation, place the company where the flow of opportunities is greatest. Simple rules then provide the guidelines within which managers can pursue such opportunities. Simple rules, which grow out of experience, fall into five broad categories: how-to rules, boundary conditions, priority rules, timing rules, and exit rules. Companies with simple-rules strategies must follow the rules religiously and avoid the temptation to change them too frequently. A consistent strategy helps managers sort through opportunities and gain short-term advantage by exploiting the attractive ones.

Gadiesh, Orit, and James L. Gilbert. "Transforming Corner-Office Strategy into Frontline Action." *Harvard Business Review*, May 2001. In addition to a strategic plan and companywide meetings, organizations use other channels to communicate their strategies to managers and employees. One of these channels is called a strategic principle—a memorable, action-oriented phrase that distills the company's strategy. Here are some examples: Southwest Airlines' "Meet customers' short-haul

travel needs at fares competitive with the cost of automobile travel";
AOL's "Consumer connectivity first—anytime, anywhere"; eBay's
"Focus on trading communities." A good strategic principle encourages
managers and employees to focus on the corporate strategy and take
risks in identifying ways to support the strategy. By communicating your
company's strategic principle frequently and consistently, you'll soon
have people throughout your organization—as well as customers and
competitors—"chanting the rant."

Kaplan, Robert S., and David P. Norton. "Using the Balanced Scorecard as
a Strategic Management System." *Harvard Business Review*, January–February 1996. The Balanced Scorecard has attracted widespread notice as a
powerful tool for clarifying and communicating strategy throughout an
organization, as well as measuring strategy implementation performance.
In this article, the authors explain how the Balanced Scorecard links
companies' short-term activities to long-term objectives through four
processes: (1) *translating the vision* by forcing managers to come to agreement on the metrics they'll need to operationalize their visions; (2) *communicating and linking* the strategy by "cascading" the top-level scorecard
down to the units and then to individuals; at each level, people identify
objectives and metrics needed to support the corporate-level scorecard;
(3) *linking strategic planning and budgeting* by ensuring that financial budgets
support strategic goals; and (4) *encouraging feedback and learning* by enabling
managers to reflect on inferences suggested by their scorecard results and
adjusting their theories about cause-and-effect relationships.

Porter, Michael E. "How Competitive Forces Shape Strategy." *Harvard
Business Review*, March–April 1979. This award-winning and highly influential article contends that many factors determine the nature of
competition, including not only rivals, but also the economics of particular industries, new entrants, the bargaining power of customers and
suppliers, and the threat of substitute services or products. A strategic
plan of action based on this model might include: positioning the company so that its capabilities provide the best defense against competitive
forces; influencing the balance of these forces through strategic moves;
and anticipating shifts in the factors underlying competitive forces.

Porter, Michael E. "Strategy and the Internet." *Harvard Business Review*,
March 2001. Many of the pioneers of Internet business, both dot-coms
and established companies, have competed in ways that violate nearly
every precept of good strategy. Rather than focus on profits, they have
chased customers indiscriminately through discounting, channel incentives, and advertising. Rather than concentrate on delivering value that
earns an attractive price from customers, they have pursued indirect revenues such as advertising and click-through fees. Rather than make

trade-offs, they have rushed to offer every conceivable product or service. It did not have to be this way—and it does not have to be in the future. When it comes to reinforcing a distinctive strategy, Porter argues, the Internet provides a better technological platform than previous generations of IT. Gaining competitive advantage does not require a radically new approach to business; it requires building on the proven principles of effective strategy. Porter also contends that, contrary to recent thought, the Internet is not disruptive to most existing industries and established companies. It rarely nullifies important sources of competitive advantage in an industry; it often makes them even more valuable. And as all companies embrace Internet technology, the Internet itself will be neutralized as a source of advantage. Robust competitive advantages will arise instead from traditional strengths such as unique products, proprietary content, and distinctive physical activities. Internet technology may be able to fortify those advantages, but it is unlikely to supplant them.

Porter, Michael E. "What Is Strategy?" *Harvard Business Review*, November–December 1996. This classic HBR article starts with the premise that today's dynamic markets and technologies have called into question the sustainability of competitive advantage. Under pressure to improve productivity, quality, and speed, managers have embraced tools such as TQM, benchmarking, and reengineering. As described by Porter, dramatic operational improvements have resulted, but rarely have these gains translated into sustainable profitability. And gradually, the tools have taken the place of strategy. As managers push to improve on all fronts, they move further away from viable competitive positions. Porter argues that operational effectiveness, although necessary to superior performance, is not sufficient, because its techniques are easy to imitate. In contrast, the essence of strategy is choosing a unique and valuable position rooted in systems of activities that are much more difficult to match.

Raffoni, Melissa. "Three Keys to Effective Execution." *Harvard Management Update*, February 2003. Execution gets little intellectual respect. In contrast, strategic planning has all the cachet and gets all the ink. Why? Because it rewards creativity, the most valued of intellectual endeavors. But experienced unit heads know that the most creative, visionary strategic planning is useless if it isn't translated into action. Think simplicity, clarity, focus—and review your progress relentlessly. Execution is what separates the companies that prosper in hard times from the ones that go under. Includes the sidebar "Books on Execution."

Van Zwieten, John. "How Not to Waste Your Investment in Strategy." *Training & Development*, June 1999. Perhaps you've experienced this in your company: The organization creates a great plan for the future but gets undesirable results when it rolls the plan into action. Managers now lack the confidence to carry out a new plan. Good strategy has apparently been defeated by bad change management. In this article, Van Zwieten explores six common dilemmas faced by executive and lower-level managers attempting to change strategic direction. He then provides a diagnosis for each dilemma and offers lessons. For example, one dilemma is characterized by divisions that are working at cross-purposes. Such companies, the author explains, likely encourage competition between divisions. The solution? An overarching vision of how divisions can cooperate, including a plan for presenting "one face" to customers. The article concludes by identifying characteristics of the most successful organizations. These include: a well-defined purpose that employees understand, a clear explanation of how the proposed change supports the purpose, shared values that guide the way business is practiced, and a "BHAG"—a "big, hairy, audacious goal" (as defined by James Collins and Jerry Porras).

Books

Aaker, David A. *Developing Business Strategies*, 6th edition. New York: John Wiley & Sons, Inc., 2001. A textbook with a practical sense, this book is designed to give managers a framework for identifying and selecting appropriate strategies. It provides a very through discussion of strategic analysis—i.e., analysis of the market, customers, and competitors. It then goes through the various categories of alternative strategic choices, including global.

Andrews, Kenneth R. *The Concept of Corporate Strategy.* Revised edition. Homewood, IL: Richard D. Irwin, Inc., 1980. First published in 1971, this is the book that started it all. Andrews defined strategy in terms of what a business could do—that is, in terms of its strengths and weaknesses—and what possibilities were open to it—that is, the outer environment of threats and opportunities. *The Concept of Corporate Strategy* remains one of the classics of modern business literature.

Barney, Jay. *Gaining and Sustaining Competitive Advantage*, 2nd edition. Upper Saddle River, NJ: Prentice Hall, 2001. A thorough treatment of the subject in college textbook form. Barney presents the core strategies and how they can be used in complementary fashion.

Bossidy, Larry, and Ram Charan. *Execution: The Discipline of Getting Things Done.* New York: Crown Business, 2002. These authors, a retired CEO and a business consultant, write that "Execution is *the* great unaddressed issue in the business world today. Its absence is the biggest single obstacle to success and the cause of most of the disappointments that are mistakenly attributed to other causes." A great strategy is insufficient for success; it must also be executed with skill. This book provides prescriptions for strategy execution.

Day, George, and David J. Reibstein. *Wharton on Dynamic Competitive Strategy.* New York: John Wiley & Sons, Inc., 1997. For the strategist, the changing external environment represents a serious challenge. This book aims to help readers rise to that challenge by offering a dynamic and integrative view of competitive strategies. These are presented in chapters written by various management professors of the Wharton School.

Fogg, C. Davis. *Implementing Your Strategic Plan: How to Turn Intent into Effective Action for Sustainable Change.* AMACOM, 1999. This book lays out the steps required to understand your company's strategy and strategic plan, develop a unit plan, and implement your unit plan. Fogg organizes the book around eighteen keys to successful implementation of a plan. These include establishing accountability; turning strategic priorities into assigned, measurable action plans; fostering creative leadership and mental toughness; removing resistance; allocating resources effectively; empowering employees; and communicating strategy to everyone, all the time. The book includes a wealth of examples, practical advice, and techniques for turning strategic plans into reality. Though aimed at senior managers, it offers lessons for managers and team leaders at every level of an organization.

Fogg, C. Davis. *Team-Based Strategic Planning: A Complete Guide to Structuring, Facilitating, and Implementing the Process.* AMACOM, 1994. Fogg focuses on strategic planning in a team environment, exploring six key aspects: (1) structure and customization—designing the planning process to meet the needs of your organization, (2) facilitation—making things happen, from running meetings to documenting decisions, (3) teamwork—building teams and resolving conflicts, (4) leadership—forging the vision and making the plan operational, (5) organizational involvement—gaining commitment at all levels, and (6) information gathering and analysis—benchmarking, competitive analyses, and other valuable techniques. Examples from actual companies illustrate each step of the process, and case studies reveal what worked and what didn't. The book also includes hands-on tools for mastering the strategic planning process.

Kieffer, David, Haig Nalbantian, Rick Guzzo, and Jay Doherty. *Playing to Your Strengths.* New York: McGraw Hill Publishing Company, 2003. Few executives take the time to examine the alignment between their business strategies and their people practices and policies. These authors explain how misalignment here can jeopardize the success of even the best strategy. Their research describes several companies whose promotion, retention, and rewards practices were inadvertently encouraging employee behaviors contrary to strategic intentions. In one case, a U.S. manufacturer's policy of building general management skills through frequent, short-term job assignments was undermining its higher goals of product quality and bringing new models to market quickly. Analysis indicated that managers who accepted short-term assignments were rewarded with promotions and higher pay, but they failed to build the technical skills needed to advance the company's higher-level strategy.

Markides, Constantinos C. *All the Right Moves: A Guide to Crafting Breakthrough Strategy*. Boston: Harvard Business School Press, 2000. Markides explores the key questions companies must answer to define a strategy: "Who should we target as customers? What products or services should we offer them? How should we do this efficiently? How can we differentiate ourselves from rivals to stake out a unique competitive position?" But even the best strategies have a limited life. Companies must continually create new strategic positions—often by breaking the rules of the game. *All the Right Moves* reveals how creative thinking—including examining an issue from a variety of angles and experimenting with new ideas—leads to strategic innovation. Strategy formulation also requires companies to make tough choices. This book offers concrete advice for thinking through those choices—systematically and successfully.

Pascale, Richard T., and Anthony G. Athos. *The Art of Japanese Management*. New York: Simon & Schuster, 1981. Though currently out of print, this 1980s classic is still available on the Web and still speaks to the importance of excellence in implementation. The authors take a hard look at two corporations—one American and one Japanese—and explain why the Japanese company had become so much more productive.

Pascale, Richard T. *Managing on the Edge: Companies That Use Conflict to Stay Ahead*. New York: Simon & Schuster, 1990. Pascale, an academic and consultant, is concerned with corporate renewal. He recommends that executives attend to four internal principles to keep their companies at the top of their games. These are: fit, split, contend, and transcend. *Fit* describes the corporation's internal consistency; *split* refers to the wisdom of reducing big organizations into smaller more manageable units; *contend* refers to the inevitable organizational contradictions that must be managed. Leaders must also *transcend* the complexity that afflicts every business.

Porter, Michael E. *Competitive Strategy*. New York: Free Press, 1980. This is the granddaddy of all strategy books and has influenced more business

executives around the world than any other. In explaining how to ana-
lyze the competitive situation in an industry, the author captures the
complexity of industry competition in five underlying forces. He also
explains three generic strategies—low cost, differentiation, and focus—
and demonstrates how these can help the individual firm with strategic
positioning, and how they are linked to profitability. Readers will find
his suggestions on treatment of rival firms very useful. He provides a
practical framework for predicting how competitors will respond to one's
own strategic moves. The book provides two very useful appendices:
Portfolio Techniques in Competitor Analysis, and How to Conduct an
Industry Analysis.

Yoffie, David, and May Kwak. *Judo Strategy.* Boston: Harvard Business
School Press, 2001. These authors reveal how a centuries-old strategy
can enable smaller firms to meet and defeat rivals many times their size.
At the heart of judo strategy is the premise that sheer size and raw
strength are no match for balance, skill, and flexibility. Using examples
from companies such as Wal-Mart, PalmPilot, CNET, and others, the
authors explain how to translate the three key principles of judo into a
winning business strategy: use movement to throw off your opponent's
balance; maintain your balance as you respond to attacks; and exploit
leverage to magnify your strength. Highly practical tools aid managers
in developing their own judo strategies, including identifying competitors' vulnerabilities, staking unoccupied terrain, and regaining ground
after setbacks. A warrior's manual for understanding how judo strategy
and defense can strengthen your firm, this powerful book is for both
Davids and Goliaths who want to compete and win on the new business battlefield.

Index

action plans
  action steps formulation, 84–85
  financial impact estimation, 90
  goal setting, 80–82
  interlocks identification, 86–88
  performance measures agreement,
      82–84
  resources need determination, 85–86
  sample plan, 90–92
  summary, 92–93
  tips for developing, 89
  transferring strategic goals to unit
      goals, 78–80
alignment, 64–65, 73–74
Andrews, Kenneth, xii
AOL, 53
Apple Computer, 43, 56, 130
Art of Japanese Management, The (Pascale
    and Athos), 65
Athos, Anthony, 65

balanced scorecard, 127–128, 129f
balance principle in strategy, 53
balance sheet, 123–124
Bank of America, 58
benchmarking, 19–20, 22t
Black & Decker, 35
blitzkrieg strategy, 70–71
Bossidy, Larry, 97
Bovet, David, 37
Brandenburger, Adam, 31
build-versus-buy decision, 58–59
Butterfield & Butterfield, 58

capital access and spending, 23
cash flow analysis, 23
CEMEX, 37
change resistance, 104–106
Charan, Ram, 97
Christensen, Clayton, 122
Collins, Jim, 58
Collis, David, 21, 68
commodity differentiation, 37
communication and strategy imple-
    mentation, 117–119
Concept of Corporate Strategy, The
    (Andrews), xii
continuous process improvement, 33
core competencies
  benchmarking used for assessing,
      19–20, 22t
  criteria for competing on, 21
  described, 18–19
  summary, 27–28
Corning, 19
Cracker Barrel Old Country Store, 40
cross-functional teams, 87–88
culture
  strategy implementation and, 71–74
  SWOT analysis and, 24–25
customer relationship management
    (CRM), 42
customer relationship strategy
  company example, 39–41
  focus strategy, 40
  value seen in the relationship, 38
  ways to add value, 41–42

customers
  in external SWOT analysis, 6–8
  price sensitivity of, 8–11
  relationship with (*see* customer relationship strategy)

Day, George, 11
Dell, 34–35
differentiation strategy
  of a commodity product, 37
  company examples, 36–37
  effectiveness of, 37–38
  as a strategic move, xii–xiii, 54–55
digital cameras, 133
Drew, Dick, 72
Drucker, Peter, 6–8

Earle, Edward Mead, xii
Eastman, George, 54
eBay, xiii, xv–xvi, 43, 58
Edison, Thomas, 36
E.J. Korvette, 31
elasticity of demand, 8–11
executing a strategic plan
  common causes of failure, 102–106
  contingency planning, 106–107
  flow chart for troubleshooting, 97*f*
  performance measures use, 100 (*see also* strategy performance measurement)
  progress reviews, 98–101, 140
  quarterly reviews, 100
  senior management and, 101–102
  summary, 108
  tools for monitoring a plan, 98
experience curve exploitation, 33–34

Fidelity, 41
financial analysis
  action plan impact estimation, 90
  to evaluate strategy effectiveness, 123–126
  in SWOT analysis, 23–24
five forces framework, 13–14
Fleet Bank, 58
Freeserve, 53

General Electric, xiv, 114
General Motors (GM), 24
Gertz, Dwight, 66
goals, implementing, 78–82

Henderson, Bruce, xii
Herman Miller, Inc., 62–64, 71, 113–114
"How Competitive Forces Shape Strategy" (Porter), 13
human resources and strategy. *See* people side of implementation
hurdle rate in SWOT analysis, 23

IBM, 56
IDC, 4–5
incentives and rewards, 66–68, 115
income statement, 124
intellectual property, 54
interlocks identification, 86–88, 104
iPod, 56–57, 130

judo strategy, 52–54

kaizen, 33
Kaplan, Robert, 127
Keynes, John Maynard, 134
Kmart, 31
Kodak, 54, 133
Kotter, John, 112, 116
Kruse International, 58
Kwak, Mary, 52, 53

Labovitz, George, 64
Land, Edwin, 54
leadership and change
  company culture and, 71–74
  senior management's need to be involved, 101–102
  strategy performance measurement and, 134–135
leverage principle in strategy, 53
L.L. Bean, 19
low-cost leadership strategy
  company examples, 31
  continuous process improvement and, 33

experience curve exploitation, 33–34
key to success, 31–32, 36
product redesign, 35
service sector and, 32–33
supply chain economies, 34–35

Magretta, Joan, xv
market analysis, 128–130
market beachhead, 48–50
market segmentation, 7
Martha, Joseph, 37
McKnight, William, 72
Mercer Human Resources Consulting,
    68
Microsoft, 43
milestones celebration, 115–116
Minnetonka Corporation, 54–55
Montgomery, Cynthia, 21, 68
Motorola, 114
movement principle in strategy,
    52–53

network effect strategy, 42–43
Norton, David, 127
Nucor Corporation, 51

Omidyar, Pierre, 43
operating margin, 126
O'Reilly, Charles, 111

Pascale, Richard, 65
patents, 54
people side of implementation
    communication, 117–119
    consistency in behaviors and mes-
        sages, 113–114
    enabling structures and, 114–115
    milestones celebration, 115–116
    misalignments in incentives, 66–68
    selecting team members, 111–112
    summary, 120
performance measures, 82–84, 100
Pfeffer, Jeffrey, 64
Pilkington Glass, 51
Polaroid, 54
Porsche, 36–37

Porter, Michael, xii, xiii, 3, 13, 40, 44,
    68, 123
price sensitivity of customers, 8–11
process reengineering, 33
Procter & Gamble, 53
profitability ratios, 125–126
proprietary methods, 54

quarterly reviews, 100

resistance to change, 104–106
return on assets, 125
return on equity, 125–126
reward systems, 66–68, 115
Rosansky, Victor, 64

"Say-Do Problem," 67, 68
segmentation, market, 7
senior management involvement,
    101–102
service sector and low-cost leadership,
    32–33
Seven S Framework, 65
Société Micromécanique et Horlogère,
    35
Sony, 18, 55–56
Southwest Airlines, xiii, 68–70
steel industry, 51
strategic moves
    buying your way in, 57–59
    judo strategy use, 52–54
    market beachhead, gaining, 48–50
    new market creation and domina-
        tion, 55–57
    process innovation use, 50–51
    product differentiation use, 54–55
    summary, 59–60
strategy
    approaches to (see strategic moves)
    business model versus, xiv–xvi
    creation process, xv–xviii
    defined, xi–xii, xiv
    follow through (see executing a
        strategic plan)
    implementing (see strategy
        implementation)

strategy, *continued*
  measuring success (*see* strategy
      performance measurement)
  types (*see* strategy types)
strategy implementation
  action plans for (*see* action plans)
  alignment and, 64–65, 73–74
  company example, 62–64
  culture and leadership and, 71–74
  organizational structure and, 70–71
  people and (*see* people side of
      implementation)
  post-implementation (*see* executing
      a strategic plan)
  project progress report, 140
  strategy creation versus, 63
  summary, 75
  supportive activities and, 68–70
strategy performance measurement
  balanced scorecard, 127–128, 129*f*
  financial analysis, 123–126
  leading change, 134–135
  market analysis, 128–130
  new competitors as a warning sign,
      130–132
  new technology as a warning sign,
      132–134
  summary, 135–136
  while executing a plan, 100
strategy types
  choosing a strategy, 44–45
  competitive advantage and, xii–xiii
  customer relationship (*see* customer
      relationship strategy)
  differentiation (*see* differentiation
      strategy)
  low-cost leadership (*see* low-cost
      leadership strategy)
  network effect, 42–43
  summary, 45–46
Stuart, Harborne, 31
supply chain economies, 34–35
Surowiecki, James, 25
SWOT analysis, external
  competitive analysis, 11–12
  customer identification, 6–8

customer price sensitivity, 8–11
elements, 2–3
emerging technologies, 12–13
five forces framework, 13–14
relating a company to its environ-
    ment, 3–4
summary, 15
worksheet, 138
workstyle and lifestyle trends, 4–6
SWOT analysis, internal
  collective intelligence organization,
      25–27
  core competencies (*see* core
      competencies)
  financial condition, 23–24
  management and culture, 24–25
  strengths and weaknesses evaluation,
      25–27
  summary, 27–28
  worksheet, 138

Target, 31
teams, 87–88, 111–112
technologies, 12–13, 132–134
3M, 19, 71, 72
TIAA-CREF, 40
Toyota, xiii, 36
Tushman, Michael, 111

USAA, 19, 39–41

Vanguard Group, 32–33
Volvo, 36
von Clausewitz, Carl, xi, 48

Walman, 55–56
Wal-Mart, 31, 32, 35, 50
Walton, Sam, 50
On War (von Clausewitz), 48
winner-take-all strategy, 43
work breakdown structure, 84,
    139

Xerox, 19–20, 114

Yoffie, David, 52, 53

About the Subject Adviser

For the past eighteen years **DAVID J. COLLIS** has been a professor at the Harvard Business School, where he continues to teach and chair Executive Education programs, the Yale University School of Management, and Columbia Business School. He is currently the M.B.A. Class of 1958 Senior Lecturer in the Strategy group at the Harvard Business School, having previously completed five years as the Frederick Frank adjunct Professor of International Business Administration at the Yale School of Management. He is an expert on corporate strategy and global competition, and the author of the recent books *Corporate Strategy* (with Cynthia Montgomery) and *Corporate Headquarters* (with Michael Goold and David Young). His work has been frequently published in the *Harvard Business Review, Academy of Management Journal, Strategic Management Journal,* and *European Management Journal*; and in many books, including *Managing the Multibusiness Company, International Competitiveness,* and *Beyond Free Trade.* The more than fifty cases he has authored have sold over 400,000 copies worldwide.

Mr. Collis received an M.A. (1976) with a Double First from Cambridge University, where he was the Wrenbury Scholar of the University. He graduated as a Baker Scholar from Harvard Business School, M.B.A. (1978), and received a Ph.D. (1986) in Business Economics at Harvard University, where he was a Dean's Doctoral Fellow. From 1978 to 1982 he worked for The Boston Consulting Group in London. He is currently a consultant to several major U.S. corporations, on the board of trustees of the Hult International Business School, and on the advisory boards of WebCT, Vivaldi Partners, Folderwave, and, formerly, Ocean Spray. He is also the cofounder of the e-learning company E-Edge, and the advisory firm Ludlow Partners.

About the Writer

RICHARD LUECKE is the writer of many books in the Harvard Business Essentials series. Based in Salem, Massachusetts, Mr. Luecke has authored or developed more than forty books and dozens of articles on a wide range of business subjects. He has an M.B.A. from the University of St. Thomas. He can be reached at richard.luecke@verizon.net.

Harvard Business Review Paperback Series

The Harvard Business Review Paperback Series offers the best thinking on cutting-edge management ideas from the world's leading thinkers, researchers, and managers. Designed for leaders who believe in the power of ideas to change business, these books will be useful to managers at all levels of experience, but especially senior executives and general managers. In addition, this series is widely used in training and executive development programs.

Books are priced at $19.95 U.S.
Price subject to change.

Title	Product #
Harvard Business Review **Interviews with CEOs**	3294
Harvard Business Review on **Advances in Strategy**	8032
Harvard Business Review on **Appraising Employee Performance**	7685
Harvard Business Review on **Becoming a High Performance Manager**	1296
Harvard Business Review on **Brand Management**	1445
Harvard Business Review on **Breakthrough Leadership**	8059
Harvard Business Review on **Breakthrough Thinking**	191X
Harvard Business Review on **Building Personal and Organizational Resilience**	2721
Harvard Business Review on **Business and the Environment**	2336
Harvard Business Review on **The Business Value of IT**	9121
Harvard Business Review on **Change**	8842
Harvard Business Review on **Compensation**	701X
Harvard Business Review on **Corporate Ethics**	273X
Harvard Business Review on **Corporate Governance**	2379
Harvard Business Review on **Corporate Responsibility**	2748
Harvard Business Review on **Corporate Strategy**	1429
Harvard Business Review on **Crisis Management**	2352
Harvard Business Review on **Culture and Change**	8369
Harvard Business Review on **Customer Relationship Management**	8994

Title	Product #
Harvard Business Review on **Decision Making**	5572
Harvard Business Review on **Developing Leaders**	5003
Harvard Business Review on **Doing Business in China**	6387
Harvard Business Review on **Effective Communication**	1437
Harvard Business Review on **Entrepreneurship**	9105
Harvard Business Review on **Finding and Keeping the Best People**	5564
Harvard Business Review on **Innovation**	6145
Harvard Business Review on **The Innovative Enterprise**	130X
Harvard Business Review on **Knowledge Management**	8818
Harvard Business Review on **Leadership**	8834
Harvard Business Review on **Leadership at the Top**	2756
Harvard Business Review on **Leadership in a Changed World**	5011
Harvard Business Review on **Leading in Turbulent Times**	1806
Harvard Business Review on **Managing Diversity**	7001
Harvard Business Review on **Managing High-Tech Industries**	1828
Harvard Business Review on **Managing People**	9075
Harvard Business Review on **Managing Projects**	6395
Harvard Business Review on **Managing the Value Chain**	2344
Harvard Business Review on **Managing Uncertainty**	9083
Harvard Business Review on **Managing Your Career**	1318
Harvard Business Review on **Marketing**	8040
Harvard Business Review on **Measuring Corporate Performance**	8826
Harvard Business Review on **Mergers and Acquisitions**	5556
Harvard Business Review on **Mind of the Leader**	6409
Harvard Business Review on **Motivating People**	1326
Harvard Business Review on **Negotiation**	2360
Harvard Business Review on **Nonprofits**	9091
Harvard Business Review on **Organizational Learning**	6153
Harvard Business Review on **Strategic Alliances**	1334
Harvard Business Review on **Strategies for Growth**	8850
Harvard Business Review on **Teams That Succeed**	502X
Harvard Business Review on **Turnarounds**	6366
Harvard Business Review on **What Makes a Leader**	6374
Harvard Business Review on **Work and Life Balance**	3286

Harvard Business Essentials

In the fast-paced world of business today, everyone needs a personal resource—a place to go for advice, coaching, background information, or answers. The Harvard Business Essentials series fits the bill. Concise and straightforward, these books provide highly practical advice for readers at all levels of experience. Whether you are a new manager interested in expanding your skills or an experienced executive looking to stay on top, these solution-oriented books give you the reliable tips and tools you need to improve your performance and get the job done. Harvard Business Essentials titles will quickly become your constant companions and trusted guides.

These books are priced at $19.95 U.S., except as noted.
Price subject to change.

Title	Product #
Harvard Business Essentials: **Negotiation**	1113
Harvard Business Essentials: **Managing Creativity and Innovation**	1121
Harvard Business Essentials: **Managing Change and Transition**	8741
Harvard Business Essentials: **Hiring and Keeping the Best People**	875X
Harvard Business Essentials: **Finance for Managers**	8768
Harvard Business Essentials: **Business Communication**	113X
Harvard Business Essentials: **Manager's Toolkit ($24.95)**	2896
Harvard Business Essentials: **Managing Projects Large and Small**	3213
Harvard Business Essentials: **Creating Teams with an Edge**	290X
Harvard Business Essentials: **Entrepreneur's Toolkit**	4368
Harvard Business Essentials: **Coaching and Mentoring**	435X
Harvard Business Essentials: **Crisis Management**	4376
Harvard Business Essentials: **Time Management**	6336
Harvard Business Essentials: **Power, Influence, and Persuasion**	631X
Harvard Business Essentials: **Strategy**	6328

The Results-Driven Manager

The Results-Driven Manager series collects timely articles from Harvard Management Update and Harvard Management Communication Letter to help senior to middle managers sharpen their skills, increase their effectiveness, and gain a competitive edge. Presented in a concise, accessible format to save managers valuable time, these books offer authoritative insights and techniques for improving job performance and achieving immediate results.

These books are priced at $14.95 U.S.
Price subject to change.

Title	Product #
The Results-Driven Manager:	
Face-to-Face Communications for Clarity and Impact	3477
The Results-Driven Manager:	
Managing Yourself for the Career You Want	3469
The Results-Driven Manager:	
Presentations That Persuade and Motivate	3493
The Results-Driven Manager: **Teams That Click**	3507
The Results-Driven Manager:	
Winning Negotiations That Preserve Relationships	3485
The Results-Driven Manager: **Dealing with Difficult People**	6344
The Results-Driven Manager: **Taking Control of Your Time**	6352
The Results-Driven Manager: **Getting People on Board**	6360
The Results-Driven Manager:	
Motivating People for Improved Performance	7790
The Results-Driven Manager: **Becoming an Effective Leader**	7804
The Results-Driven Manager:	
Managing Change to Reduce Resistance	7812

How to Order

Harvard Business School Press publications are available worldwide from your local bookseller or online retailer.
You can also call

1-800-668-6780

Our product consultants are available to help you
8:00 a.m.–6:00 p.m., Monday–Friday, Eastern Time.
Outside the U.S. and Canada, call: 617-783-7450
Please call about special discounts for quantities greater than ten.

You can order online at

www.HBSPress.org